WORLD WAR 1

The Sacrifice of a Generation

CONTENTS

INTRODUCTION

IT IS ALWAYS A TRUE challenge for any historian and writer to begin tackling a subject so large in scope and significance. When considered today, more than a century later, the First World War can be studied in significant detail, and explored in every aspect. But when you attempt to write about it and deliver a concise picture of this crucial period of the World's history, you are quickly faced with your very first challenge: even before the first word has been put down. And that challenge is this: how can you portray with due justice a conflict of such magnitude – the first true *World War*?

How to reflect on the millions of lives lost in the whirlwind of global conflict and deliver an unbiased and thorough book that will give due respect to all those whose lives were lost forever in the many war-torn corners of the world?

As a writer and a passionate historian, I placed this big challenge as my guiding line – even before I began writing this work. In order to deliver the vision of the First World War that *needs* to be seen, to be known and remembered for generations to come. Because even when the final outcome of a war is *victory*, it cannot be gained without sacrifice and defeats along the way. With that being said, this work will attempt to reflect on all the aspects of this all-encompassing, global war. From the trenches of the Western Front, all the way to the sweeping hand-to-hand battles of the Balkan Front, the human sacrifice needs to be addressed. Still, there is another critical viewpoint that needs to be taken when tackling such a wide subject. And that viewpoint is *dialogue*. We need to observe a global conflict that is today more than a century old, and view its causes and its after effects from a modern, contemporary point of view.

This Great War has been discussed and explained by generations of historians – and we, today, can reflect upon all their collected work and use it as a source for creating a refined and thorough work of history literature.

A lot has changed since that turbulent first decade of the 20th century, and history was restless ever since – and never the same. But never did it come close to the scale and brutality of that great old macabre giant that is the First World War. In the age of venerable and failing monarchies, in a time where the old traditions faced modern technologies, in the world where oppressed nations cried in unison for their freedoms – the world held its breath. From those early months of 1914, the entire globe waited fearfully and impatiently, as Europe see-sawed over an abyss of warfare.

But, alas, the tides of war could not be avoided – Europe plunged into war, and the world followed closely behind. What started as a conflict between two nations brewed up into the first true global conflict, later to be known as the *Great War*, and then the World War. It lasted from 28th of July 1914, to 11th November 1918, and claimed millions upon millions of lives in the process. Today, the First World War is regarded as one of the deadliest conflicts in human history, and one that came at a grave cost for Europe – whose 60 million sons and daughters marched into the flames of war.

World War One was the war of firsts in many other important regards as well. It came at a crucial turning point in the world – a time when large scale industry was coming to the forefront, and old traditions were rapidly fading out. And this industry quickly became militarized, bringing new changes into the traditional methods of warfare that were long established up to that point. And with that, everything became up-scaled: large scale warfare and devastating new weapons led to large scale deaths. Frontlines became large, and warfare spread quickly from the ground to the air, and then to the sea. In many regards, it became the war that brought out the worst in man. Long gone were the days of chivalry and respect between enemies. Long forgotten were the days of duels and honor and face to face warfare on the open field. The First World War ushered the world into an age of airplanes and bombardment, of attrition warfare and starvation. It pushed the world face first into the mud of far spreading trenches, of poisonous gas warfare and aerial supremacy. Yes, it was a war of firsts, and the big gate through which the world fell one whole step down –never to climb back up again. And today, so many years later, we can at last see that after the First World War, the world was never again the same.

CHAPTER I
SETTING THE STAGE
FOR WAR: THE
BACKGROUND

BEFORE DIVING IN DIRECTLY into the causes and crucial events that led to the war itself, it is important to first reflect on the important changes and developments that the world was facing with the coming of the 20th century. These changes were often highly dynamic and somewhat uneven. And one of the most important was industry. At first, the large scale industries were reserved for urban centers, while the rural areas continued with their age old way of life. But soon enough, this too was to change. The focus quickly shifted towards rapid industrialization, and with that, many other aspects changed.

With the onset of industry came urbanization and the rise of the metropolitan areas and major urban centers. This directly led to a major shift in demographics all around Europe. The gradual emergence of large corporations and factories, all of which employed thousands of workers, and with the shift from steam engines to petrol, it was clear that Europe and the rest of the world were heading into a new age where the old ways of rural life were quickly fading out.

Another crucial change that the world experienced relates to *demographics.* At the beginning of the century Europe experienced a real population boom. Large migrations took place during the first years of the 20th century, motivated by the call for work force by the large industries, and many Europeans found themselves on the shores of North America, in search of a brighter future and better work. Those that remained in their countries in Europe also saw the numerous opportunities that arose in towns. Movements began towards urban centers and developing communities, and many cities rapidly grew in no more than a decade. This rapid change was the biggest contributor to a significant class difference: the growing industries and commerce was a new source of wealth, and from it rose a professional, commercial, white collar middle class. On the other hand, the rise in population and the shift from established rural lifestyles into the rapidly growing cities still resulted in substantial levels of poverty for the lower class, blue collar working families. These working class families often had around four children on average, and had to live in under-developed apartment blocks in often squalid conditions. The great gap between the classes was gradually becoming quite apparent – in every aspect of life in the early 20th century. Segregation in urban environments became increased, with a great difference in dress and social habits of the rich and poor.

1.1 - The Race to Power

The leading power in the so-called *"Industrial Revolution"* of the mid 19th century was Britain, which rose to become the leading industrial giant of the world, often called the *"world's workshop"*. However, other European powers soon began catching up, creating a certain race towards power and wealth. By 1870's, Germany rapidly expanded its industries and became the leading producer of coal, steel, and iron, and by 1913, it has replaced Britain in its position of industrial dominance. Outside of Europe, USA held the title of the biggest industrial power on the planet – uncontested.

However, a big imbalance was created in Europe. Smaller nations struggled to compete and to parallel the rapid growth of Germany, and this imbalance between power levels was soon too great to be mended. And it was this enormous difference in power levels that would have very serious and very palpable implications later on.

Nationalism also got on the rise in the late stages of the 19th century and onwards. For the governments of the leading powers, this was a sure way of winning over the citizens, ensuring the votes, and guiding the working classes towards a patriotic direction. It was also a proven way to smoothen out the growing gap between the classes – a gap that was appearing in much of Europe. It efficiently connected all the classes and drew them together if the security of their nation ever came into question. Imperialism, nationalism, and patriotism, were all highly efficient tools that ensured that even the lowest impoverished classes shared the same interests as did the nation itself.

For much of the late 19th century, the leading nations of Europe struggled to maintain a shaky balance between them. This struggle led to the creation of numerous complicated military alliances and trade deals. The aged German chancellor Otto Von Bismarck, at the head of the leading power, sought to maintain peace by preserving this balance. He did so by holding all the competing powers in check – he arbitrated the dealings between Russia and Austria-Hungary, and kept France in diplomatic isolation, without significant allies. He was the creator of several highly important and ingenious treaties and alliances which benefited both Europe and Germany. One of these was the *Reinsurance Treaty*, in effect from 1897 to 1890, a diplomatic agreement between Russia and Germany, ensuring their neutrality in case either entered a war with a major power. This treaty was sadly one of the last assurances of peace in Europe: as soon as Bismarck resigned from his position in 1890, his policies and his work were soon to be gone.

The Reinsurance Treaty was almost immediately allowed to lapse and become redundant, and was replaced by the *Dual Alliance,* a defensive treaty between Germany and Austria-Hungary. Soon after, the alliance was further expanded, and Italy was included in the treaty. This was all the work of Bismarck's unskilled successor, the new Chancellor Leo Von Caprivi, who greatly lacked the diplomatic and nation-leading abilities of his predecessor.

The truth was that the powers of Europe all relied on a network of allies, whose alliance would then act as a certain "safety" against war. This fact gave Russia the initiative to seek out a new ally, after Germany opted for their new Triple Alliance. This resulted in the Franco-Russian Alliance that would last from 1891 to 1914. This alliance would then include Great Britain as well, resulting in the forming of the Triple Entente. Thus were created two opposing alliance blocks, with allies that felt obliged to provide aid to one another in case of war. And that created one of the biggest contributions to the war that was about to break out.

Starting in the final years of the 19th century and spilling over into the 20th, the rivalry between Germany and Great Britain took on an even bigger scope. The escalating race to power in Europe, and the accompanying deterioration of their bilateral relations, caused an *arms race* between these two powers. This arms race soon got focused on the *naval* aspect: In 1897 the German Admiral, Alfred Von Tirpitz, began the Anglo-German Naval Race with his plan to create a formidable naval force that would challenge Britain and force it to make *diplomatic concessions.* But in actuality, this German navy would be a "fleet in being" – meaning that it was a fleet to exert a controlling influence only while it is *in port.* The truth was that such a fleet could not have the certainty of victory in case of a naval conflict.

Tirpitz, the naval secretary of Kaiser Wilhelm II, was convinced that naval dominance was the certain way of gaining leverage against Great Britain in the political sphere. Enthusiastic about the German expansion overseas and naval power, the Kaiser approved of Tirpitz's plan and placed it into motion.

The German Reich Navy Office thus began implementing a long-term process of expanding the German fleet, with the end goal being no less than 60 big battleships. The new age of naval warfare dictated a different approach to maritime conflict: the emphasis was placed on tonnage, size, and high caliber armament.

Swiftness and raids were no longer the focus – instead it was all about the sheer bulk and size, and the ability to withstand enemy fire as long as possible.

Either way, not in the least surprisingly, the new naval expansion program was putting a lot of strain on Germany's economy and infrastructure. In 1908, the German Reichstag passed a fourth naval bill, increasing the rate of production to four battleships per year. But with the emergence of the Bosnian Crisis in that same year, most of German funds were relocated to the military. The German Chancellor, Bernhard Von Bülow, came to a conclusion that the nation could not manage to maintain both the largest military in Europe and the largest navy. This placed Tirpitz's original plan into question.

Meanwhile, the British Government had mostly ignored the naval buildup in Germany, but the potential threat was becoming more and more noticed in the inner political circles. The tensions gradually grew and the German naval expansion reached the general public, following 1908 report by the British Naval attaché from Berlin which focused on the Germany's increase in rate of battleship building. This eventually turned into a broad plea for the creation of additional dreadnought ships for the British navy, from both the public and the parts of the government. Thus it was, that starting in 1909, the British Prime Minister, Herbert Henry Asquith, proposed a compromise through which the next year would see the beginning of the production of four dreadnoughts per year. The funding for these ships was eventually passed and approved with the so-called *People's Budget*, in 1910.

In the long run, the arms race was not a success for Germany, and in 1914 they were still lacking in overall tonnage of ships, boasting just 1,019,000 tons and 17 dreadnought battleships, compared to Britain's 29 vessels and 2,205,000 tones.

1.2 - The Bosnian Crisis and the Path to War

The next major turbulent event that deepened the already present crisis in Europe was the so-called *Bosnian Crisis* of 1908. The ethnic tensions and rise of patriotic, nationalistic tendencies were already running rampant across the continent, and were particularly visible in the Balkans – an area with centuries-old multi-ethnic and multi-religious background. So, it was no surprise that tensions spiked when Austria-Hungary decided to unilaterally annex Bosnia and Herzegovina, a territory previously occupied by the Ottoman Empire.

The area already fell under strong Austro-Hungarian influence as early as 1878, following the Russian conflict with the Ottomans and a series of uprisings against their rule in the Balkans. Austria-Hungary laid its claim on Bosnia in the so-called *Budapest Conventions of 1877*, a secret agreement between Russia and Austria-Hungary, which was aimed at their division of territories and power in the Balkans and Eastern Europe.

The annexation that happened in 1908 was timed perfectly and intently with the Bulgarian Declaration of Independence from the Ottoman Empire, which also occurred in October 1908. The event sparked great protests from all Great Powers, and especially from Austria-Hungary's closest neighbors, Serbia and Montenegro. The annexation greatly strained the relations between Austria and its allies, and immensely cooled their relation with Serbia and other Slavic ethnicities, especially those in occupied Bosnia. Russia, a staunch protector and ally of its Orthodox and Slavic brother-nation Serbia, was also angered. The Balkans then quickly gained the epithet of being the "powder keg of Europe".

Before this, the Ottoman rule in the Balkans, which lasted unopposed for roughly five centuries, was seriously shaken after a series of fierce rebellions and rise in nationalism. The most important of these conflicts were the Serbian-Turkish Wars of 1876-1878, also known as the *Serbian Wars for Independence*. The wars were preceded by a Serbian uprising of 1875 in Herzegovina, a spark that turned out into a flame of Christian revolts across the Balkans. This was followed by Serbia declaring war on the Ottoman Empire on June 28th, 1876. The initial operations were focused on modern-day Southern Serbia and were marked by a string of defeats and retreats for the Serbian side. Following these initial losses, Serbian government petitioned the major European powers to be a mediator for a diplomatic solution to the conflict. This resulted in just a month of truce, after which the war continued. Nevertheless, Serbia once more made no progress against the dug-in Turks. Their dire situation saw the involvement of Russia, which threatened to enter the war against the Ottomans if they did not sign a truce. This ultimatum effectively ended the first Serbian-Turkish war.

Soon after, Russia gave major financial and military aid to Serbia, and the latter renewed the conflict in 1877, bringing it into the second phase, known as the second war. Lasting roughly two months, the second phase resulted in a decisive Serbian victory, with which they freed big parts of their southern lands and expelled many Turks and other Muslim inhabitants from these regions. After the war, their outcome was dictated by the *Congress of Berlin* in 1878 led by the German Chancellor Otto Von Bismarck, through which Serbia gained territorial expansion and an international recognition as an independent state. However, the Congress did not bring any long lasting solutions. Tensions between Russia and Austria-Hungary only escalated further, and the Balkans were not stabilized. The First and Second Balkan Wars followed just a few years after, and brought to the overall European instability in the wake of the Great War.

CHAPTER II
The Spark to Start the Flame:
The Sarajevo Assassination

2.1 – The Wars in the Balkans

THE RISE OF SLAV NATIONALISM in the Balkans was a great burden for Austria-Hungary, one which they had great issues dealing with. The displeasure was most evident in the sizeable populations of Serbs in occupied regions outside Serbia proper, who suffered centuries of occupation. Serbs lived in these areas for centuries before that: Montenegro, Dalmatia, Croatian Military Frontier, Žumberak Mountains, and Bosnia. Theirs was the loudest voice of discontent, bolstered further by other smaller South Slavic ethnicities. The Balkan region saw further destabilization even after 1908, with the onset of the *First Balkan War* of 1912-1913, which saw the Balkan nations allied as the *Balkan League* fighting against the weakened and fragmented Ottoman Empire.

The Balkan wars were a colossal disaster for the Ottomans, who already weakened in the decades before and popularly called the "*sick man of Europe*", could not even dream of retaining power and stability in the region. The so-called Balkan League consisted of Serbia, Bulgaria, Greece, and Montenegro, who were supported by Russia and a number of Italian volunteers. On the other hand, the Ottoman Empire was supported by Austria-Hungary.

The fragile Balkan League was connected simply by the promise of territorial expansion for all of the states involved in it, and not much else. Europe's major powers tried without any success to avert this conflict and stabilize the region, and by September, the armies on both sides have been mobilized. Lasting from October 1912 to May 1913, the First war was marked with rapid, landslide successes of the Balkan League. Although numerically inferior in the start, the League had hefty strategic advantages over the Ottomans. Although costly in casualties for all involved parties, the war was nonetheless a complete victory of the Balkan League, and a complete failure for the Ottomans in Europe. The latter lost an incredible 83% of territories in Europe, and more than half of its European populace.

The *Second Balkan War* followed immediately after, in 1913, and lasted only 33 days. It erupted after Bulgaria – unhappy with its territorial gains – turned against its former allies Serbia and Greece, and declared war. The region of Macedonia was the main source of dissatisfaction, half of which was under Bulgarian influence, with the other half being the region of *Old Serbia*. Furthermore, the creation of independent Albania following the first war was a great threat and issue for the Serbs. The Bulgarians started the second war on 29th of June 1913, by starting a large scale offensive towards Greece and Serbia. Romania then entered the conflict against Bulgaria, after several territorial disputes. After a short conflict and a string of defeats, Bulgaria lost the war and several of the previously gained territories. The second war destabilized the region even further, and set the backdrop for an even larger war that could consume the whole of Europe.

2.2 – A Cry For Freedom

In the following year, a crucial event occurred that would prove to be the drop to spill over the overflowing cup: the Assassination of Archduke Franz Ferdinand. The heir presumptive to the Austro-Hungarian Empire, Franz Ferdinand, alongside his wife Sophie, Duchess of Hohenberg, visited the capital of Bosnia – Sarajevo. This occurred on 28th of June, 1914, a date of serious national and religious significance for the Serbian people.

A group of six revolutionaries conspired to assassinate the Archduke on this significant date. They were: Gavrilo Princip (*Гаврило Принцип*), Cvjetko Popović (*Цветко Поповић*), Trifko

Grabež (*Трифко Грабеж*), Muhamed Mehmedbašić (*Мухамед Мехмедбашић*), Nedeljko Čabrinović (*Недељко Чабриновић*), and Vaso Čubrilović (*Васо Чубриловић*), all members of the Yugoslavist group known as *Mlada Bosna* (Young Bosnia). The driving ideology of this revolutionary movement was the unification of all South Slav peoples (Yugo Slavs), and their deliverance from centuries of foreign oppression. The annexation of Bosnia that occurred a few years previously was one of the defining causes for displeasure amongst the activists. They believed that the assassination would help the oppressed South Slav lands break from the occupation and be joined in the pan-South Slavic nation of Yugoslavia. The six revolutionaries were secretly trained and supplied with pistols and grenades by the Serbian secret military society known as *Црна Рука* (Black Hand), whose aims were also for unification of South Slav peoples under one banner.

The Archduke and his wife, alongside the accompanying party, were riding through Sarajevo in an open topped *Gräf & Stift 28/32 PS Double Phaeton* automobile, which was the third car in the column. On the day of the procession, it was agreed that the military protection around the city would be diminished – as it was considered that a strong military presence would aggravate the loyal citizens of the town. Thus it was left for the regular city police to supply the protection, and not the army. This was just one of the several subtle flaws that were present that day, and which worked in favor of the young conspirators.

The first attempt on the Archduke's life occurred at 10:10 am: as the column of cars passed the first two assassins, Čubrilović and Mehmedbašić, they both failed to act. The column then reached Čabrinović who decided to act, and threw a hand grenade at the Archduke's car. The bomb bounced off and exploded under the following vehicle, wounding numerous bystanders but not harming the target. Čabrinović attempted suicide by swallowing cyanide and jumping into the river. Both failed: the poison was somewhat expired and merely induced vomiting, while the river was at its historic shallowest point. Nauseated and wet, he was quickly captured by the police after being severely beaten by the mob.

The Archduke's car then drove off towards the Town Hall, following the intended plan of him holding a speech there. Although visibly stressed and shaken, Franz Ferdinand did eventually deliver that speech to the crowds gathered there, taking the opportunity to mention the assassination attempt while addressing the people of Sarajevo: "*I see in you an expression of your joy at the failure of the attempt at assassination..*". What followed after was a debate between him and the members of the procession on how to proceed next. While others in the Archduke's company feared further attempts at assassination, the Governor General of Bosnia, Oskar Potiorek, insisted that the town could not possibly have more assassins in it, and that the attempt was finished. The column thus proceeded towards the town hospital, in order to visit those who were wounded less than an hour earlier.

While the intention was to avoid the city centre and to stick to the more open quay, a miscommunication between the drivers saw the column taking a wrong turn and head into the centre. After taking that dreaded turn, the column found itself exactly opposite the position of Gavrilo Princip, one of the conspirators who managed to change his position after the failed first attempt. Coincidentally taking the perfect waiting position, he saw the third car with the Archduke and his wife, approached it directly, and fired two bullets from blank point range. The first shot struck the Archduke Franz Ferdinand in the jugular vein, while the other struck his wife in the abdomen. Both of them were dead by 11:30 AM that same morning.

The political implications and the subsequent turmoil were significant in the wake of the assassination. Austria-Hungary was greatly distraught, and the following month saw the onset of the so-called *July Crisis,* a period of intense diplomatic escalations between all the major powers of Europe, which quickly drifted towards the promise of war. The crisis culminated with Austria's delivery of the *July Ultimatum* to Serbia – a series of demands which were purposefully made outrageous. The Ultimatum's role was a provocation of war with Serbia – whom Austria believed was involved in the assassination and meddling in affairs of Bosnia. After receiving the ultimatum and refusing just a single demand on the list, Serbia nonetheless ordered a complete mobilization of its army. As the ultimatum was not accepted in full, Austria ordered partial mobilization, broke off all diplomatic relations, and eventually declared war on Serbia on 28th of July, 1914, ushering the world towards a global war.

CHAPTER III
THE GREAT WAR
BEGINS–3.1 – THE
ULTIMATUM

THE SENTIMENTS IN AUSTRIA-Hungary following the assassination were largely mixed. The death of Franz Ferdinand was not mourned by many – in fact, the citizens of Vienna went about their daily lives unfazed. Even the Emperor Franz Joseph, although somewhat disturbed by his heir's death, was not affected as it was known that the two were not all that close. He went as far as to not interfere in the decision that was to be brought – he left that to his foreign minister, Leopold Berchtold and his Army Chief of Staff Franz Conrad von Hötzendorf. They, and the other ministers, saw the assassination as a fit chance to once and for all remove any pretense and interference that Serbia could have had in Bosnia, thus securing the region. For all the Austrian elite and officials, war was an all too real opportunity, one that they were not so averse to.

Thus it was that the most prevalent current in the top of Austria's government was the one of immediate war against Serbia. Feldmarschall Conrad von Hötzendorf was the foremost of these warmongers, with a desire to at once terminate Serbia as a viable opponent. He famously stated in regards to Serbia: *"If you have a poisonous adder at your heel, you stamp on its head - you don't wait for the bite".* And so the decision was soon after reached, and an ultimatum was composed. An ultimatum whose demands were quite preposterous. It was presented to the Serbian government on July 23rd, by the Austrian minister in Belgrade, Baron Giesl Von Gieslingen.

The Serbian government found itself in a no-exit situation, facing an ultimatum that was purposefully made impossible to accept. Lacking the necessary support from major allied powers, the Serbian officials, alongside the King, gave it their best effort to create a compromise, in hope not to antagonize Austria-Hungary any further. The government officials met the day after, and after a lengthy meeting, a reply was drafted. Most sources agree that their reply accepted all of the terms except one, and that one being the term #6, which demanded that Austrian police operate freely in Serbia. Other scholars argue that even though the Serbs did accept some terms, they were compromised in such a way to basically become polite and worded rejections. Either way, the nature of the ultimatum was clear from the start. Just how offending and degrading the ultimatum was for Serbia, is best illustrated by this letter, dated to 24th of July and sent to the Tsar of Russia Nicholas II, by the Serbian Regent Alexander:

"...Demands in the Austro-Hungarian ultimatum quite unnecessarily humiliate Serbia and do not comply with her dignity as an independent state...We are willing to accept those Austro-Hungarian demands that are in accordance with the status of an independent state and ones that Your Majesty would advise us to adopt. All individuals for which it is proven to have been involved in the assassination will be strictly punished by us. Certain demands can not be met without changing our constitution, and that takes time. The deadline given to us is too short...the sublime compassion Your Imperial Highness has often showed towards us, inspires great hope that your generous Slavic heart will once again hear our prayers."

After receiving Serbia's reply, and seeing that the answer was not satisfactory, Austria at once broke off all diplomatic relations with Serbia. This was followed by an immediate declaration of war – albeit in an odd way: The Austro-Hungarian government declared it via a simple telegram addressed to the Serbian Government, and signed by their Foreign Minister Berchtold. Sent on 28th of July, 1914, the telegram was short and to the point, stating the following:

> *"The royal government of Serbia having not satisfactorily answered the notice that had been handed to it by the minister of Austro-Hungary in Belgrade on the 23rd of July 1914 the imperial and royal government finds itself compelled to provide itself for its rights and interest's protection and to resort therefore to force of arms. Therefore, Austro-Hungary considers itself henceforth in state of war against Serbia. The minister of foreign affairs of Austro-Hungary Count Berchtold"*

3.2 – The Descent Into War

The descent into an all out conflict in Europe was swift and decisive. The Serbian government already expected the inevitable wrath of Austria, knowing that their ultimatum was not going to be satisfactory. In preparation, they ordered complete mobilization on the very next day. Austria-Hungary followed suit, with the Emperor Franz Joseph ordering the mobilization of full eight army corps, which was then to begin combat operations against Serbia. The public in Vienna reacted positively to the declaration of war. Meanwhile, in order to create a more decisive political stance, and to offer some semblance of support towards Serbia, Russia ordered a partial mobilization against Austria-Hungary, with the main intent being to possibly deter it from actually carrying out the attack. This was then followed by further orders from the Tsar Nicholas II, with which he definitely decided to step into the conflict between Serbia and Austria by putting his armies on general alert. Upon these steps from Russia, the German Kaiser Wilhelm II asked Tsar Nicholas II – who was coincidentally his cousin – to cancel the call for mobilization and step down. When the latter refused, Germany declared war on Russia. They also sent an ultimatum to France with demands of neutrality, in which the latter was asked not to aid Russia if it got involved in defense of Serbia.

The French ignored the demands altogether, as Germany expected it to do. Nonetheless, it desired to avoid the conflict, and urged restraint, with the French Premier Rene Viviani sending a direct message to St. Petersburg, asking that Russia abstain from any actions that would provoke the wrath with Germany. Furthermore, as a sign of their peaceful intention, the French army ordered all troops to retreat 10 kilometers (6.2 miles) inland and away from the German border. Even so, with both the British and the French advocating against an all out conflict, Germany and Austria-Hungary steadily continued their move towards war. Russia continued its mobilization, with faint assurances that it is not aimed as a prelude to war. And when the Russian partial mobilization turned into a general one, Germany reacted. Kaiser Wilhelm signed the order for the general mobilization of the German Army, with the latter immediately beginning its operations to invade Belgium and Luxembourg – a part of their plan towards the invasion of France.

War on France was officially declared by Germany on August 3rd, and on Russia two days before that, August 1st. The War on Belgium was declared on August 4th, after its King, Albert, refused to accept the ultimatum sent by Germany, in which free passage was demanded. This then drew in Great Britain, whose ambassador in Germany, Sir Edward Goschen, delivered an ultimatum to the German Ministry of Foreign Affairs, demanding an immediate end to the violation of Belgian neutrality. When this ultimatum was not accepted, Great Britain declared war on Germany, on August 4th, 1914.

Austria-Hungary then lastly declared war on Russia, on August 6th. Within just a few days, the whole of Europe's major powers were at war with one another – insinuating a war of enormous scale. The widespread calls for mobilization and volunteers across Europe meant that millions of men would be conscripted.

3.3 – The Serbian Campaign

At the outbreak of war, Serbia had noticeably fewer men than what Austria-Hungary could field. Furthermore, the Austrians were noticeably better equipped in every regard. In 1914, Austria's southern (Serbian) front was commanded by General Oskar Potiorek, and their forces included some 329 battalions, and circa

500,000 men. In comparison, the defending Serbian Army and its ally Montenegro fielded some 209 battalions, and roughly 344,000 men in total. Still, the opening stages of the campaign against Serbia would come as a surprise to all.

The so-called Serbian Campaign began almost immediately. After declaring war on 28th of July, 1914, Austria-Hungary proceeded to shell Belgrade the very next day. This occurred under the cover of darkness, when the river patrol boat, *SMS Bodrog*, sailed up the river Danube and stopped adjacent to the capital, commencing a heavy artillery bombardment around 1:00 am. These were the very first shots of the Great War.

Almost three weeks after, the eager General Potiorek commenced his attack against Serbia, motivated by a desire to knock Serbia out of the war as swiftly as possible, and before the birthday of the Emperor. Sure of his success, he commanded his entire Fifth Army, and only a small element of his Second Army, entering Serbia from the direction of northern Bosnia. The experienced Serbian commanders were surprised by the unexpected direction of this attack, but have managed to swiftly direct their forces and meet the invaders. Led by the seasoned Marshal Radomir Putnik, the Serbian army faced the Austro-Hungarians in hilly western Serbia, on the *Cer* Mountain. During a harsh four day battle, lasting from 15th to the 24th of August, the Austro-Hungarians were greeted by a proper surprise.

The first clash in this decisive battle occurred during the cover of night – and almost by accident, when the forward elements of the 1st Combined Division of the Serbian army encountered Austro-Hungarian outposts. What started out as light clashes soon erupted into a fierce battle on a stretched frontline.

Veterancy quickly became a defining factor of the battle's flow. The largely inexperienced Austrian soldiers were quick to flee under the decisive and fierce attacks of battle hardened Serbian soldiers. Major clashes occurred in the retaking of the surrounding towns – Kosanin Grad and Šabac. The former was subject to repeated attacks by the Serbs, which were continually repulsed by the dug-in Austrians. However, with the pressures mounting through the night, the town was finally recaptured by the Serbs on August 19th. After several other decisive Serbian attacks along the front, the Austro-Hungarian morale suddenly collapsed, as the army began a panicked and disorderly retreat all along the frontline. The Serbian High Command ordered the pursuit of the enemy, further adding to the panic that reigned amongst the Austrian ranks. During their flight across the River Drina and back into Bosnia, many Austrian soldiers drowned.

Šabac was the only remaining goal for the Serbs – it was still defended and heavy clashes occurred in its outskirts. During 21st and 22nd of August, heavy fighting took its toll on both sides, but the Serbs prevailed. Even before they could utilize their heavy siege artillery, the Austro-Hungarians broke and fled from the city. This concluded the Battle of Cer. This was the first battle of the Great War, and the first allied victory as well. The defeat came as a sharp and embarrassing surprise for Potiorek, who was so sure of his advantages. But the Serbian soldiers were seasoned veterans of several recent wars in the Balkans, and were led by skilled cadre of commanding generals. News quickly spread all around the world, with Allies relying on the news to boost the morale of the public and the army: A small and struggling rural nation of the Balkans thoroughly devastated the prideful Austro-Hungarians!

However, celebrations were short lived. Everyone knew deep down that Serbia could not possible hope to indefinitely stave off enemy offensives. Austro-Hungarians, although embarrassingly defeated, were superior in their manpower and their armament. This became obvious in the next engagement that followed, the Battle of Drina. Fought between September 6th and October 4th 1914, it was a renewed and fiercer offensive by the Austrians, putting the Serbian Army to the test. The Battle of Drina was a series of heavy clashes, all of which exacted a heavy toll on both the invaders and the defenders. In the end, the Serbs were forced to go on a series of retreats, falling far back after the capture of Valjevo, a significant Serbian town. Still, the Serbs chose to regroup and react – leading to the Battle of Kolubara immediately afterwards. It was fought between 16th November and 15th December 1914.

The Serbs were forced to abandon their capital, Belgrade, on November 29th, and it was promptly occupied by the Austro-Hungarians. However, the Serbian army opted for a daring and surprising counter-attack along the entire line of the front. Once more the Austrians were taken aback, being unable to properly react and withstand the Serbian attacks. Major cities were liberated, and eventually the capital was freed as well. Battle of Kolubara was a decisive Serbian victory and another embarrassment for the Austrians. So much was this a failure for their army, that the Austrian Commander Oskar Potiorek was immediately relieved of command. The reason was "a most ignominious, rankling and derisory defeat".

On the other hand, Serbia entered the spotlight. It drew the attention from correspondents all over the world, and many visitors from abroad entered the country, glorifying its fighting spirit.

Nevertheless, the Serbs could not feel the happiness the others did: not only was this opening stage of the war costly in resources and manpower, but the winter also brought a debilitating typhus epidemic which claimed hundreds of thousands of lives in Serbia. This situation worsened even further in 1915. The central powers, mainly Germany and Austria-Hungary, emphasized the importance of conquering Serbia: it was a vital route towards the Ottoman Empire, and it could be crucial for the outcome of war. Thus it was that October 1915 saw a renewed series of offensives against the weakened Serbian army. The Germans and Austrians pressed towards Belgrade, and it was clear that this time, victory for the Serbs was near impossible. And then, when the Bulgarians suddenly and surprisingly attacked the Serbs from the back, the situation turned dire. Serbian armies were threatened with full encirclement and destruction, and that was reason enough for the High Command to order the *Great Retreat*.

Hundreds of thousands of Serbian soldiers and accompanying civilians fled south in an attempt to reach the coasts of the

Adriatic Sea and the allied navies that awaited there. The retreat was an ordeal of great proportions, one that remained etched in the fibre of the Serbian nation, as one of its greatest struggles. Challenged by the constant bad weather and near-impassable roads, the long columns suffered many casualties along the way. The most infamous part of this retreat was the traversing of the inhospitable Albanian mountains, where the retreating columns were decimated by the freezing winter conditions and sporadic attacks of remote Albanian tribesmen. The Great Retreat claimed many lives: over 160,000 civilians died, and the soldiers suffered 77,455 dead and 77,278 missing.

Once reaching the coasts of the Adriatic, the Serbs were evacuated by Allied ships to the Greek island of Corfu, and the Serbian government-in-exile that was established there. Even after direct danger was gone, diseases and malnutrition claimed further 11,000 Serbian lives on Corfu. Many would receive burial at sea.

In 1916, the remnants of the Serbian army would join up with the Allied Powers and fight in the crucial breakthrough of the Salonica Front.

There is no doubt that the fate of Serbia was one of hardships and constant challenges. Its resources depleted by decades of wars even before the Great War started, it was simply relying on its indomitable fighting spirit to stand up to the superior enemy threatened its sacred doorstep. The Great Retreat is remembered as one of the greatest sacrifices in Serbian history, and has often been cited by leading scholars as one of the worst tragedies of the First World War.

CHAPTER IV
THE WESTERN FRONT

4.1 – The Schlieffen Plan is Put Into Motion

ALMOST IMMEDIATELY after declaring war on France, Germany put into motion its long present plan of invading it. The campaign began on August 4th 1914, just a few days after Belgium announced that it will remain neutral in case of war, and will deny free passage to Germany. The German plan for the conquest of France was created long before that. Known as the *Schlieffen Plan,* after the man who created it, Field Marschall Graf Alfred Von Schlieffen, it was a strategic attempt to fool the French and outflank them. A similar approach will be undertaken several decades after, in the Second World War.

The core of the Schlieffen plan was centered on a wide sweeping flanking maneuver, with which they would bypass the core of the French army, capture Paris, and strike the enemy in the rear, trapping it and eliminating France from the war as rapidly as possible. Before the onset of war, the Germans thus situated approximately 80% of its army towards the West and the French border. To achieve this plan, the Germans first invaded Luxembourg on August 2nd 1914, violating its neutrality and rapidly sweeping through this small nation. It fell without any opposition. Just two days later, Belgium was attacked fiercely by the armies of Generals von Bülow and von Kluck. The next day, August 5th, saw the devastating Battle of Liège, which lasted until August 16th and ended in a victory for the Germans. Both sides suffered heavy casualties. Afterwards, most of the Belgian army retreated, and Belgium was effectively conquered by August 23rd. During its occupation, numerous radical policies by the Germans were introduced, and many atrocities committed, in what was to become the so-called *"Rape of Belgium"*.

After their conquest of both Luxembourg and Belgium, the next stage of the Schlieffen Plan was ready to be executed. Just as was planed, the German army entered the north of France, where they were met by the combined armies of the French and the British Expeditionary Force. What resulted next was a series of heavy battles, which collectively became known as the *Battle of the Frontiers.* This series of clashes lasted from August 7th to September 6th 1914, and was very costly in manpower for all sides involved. Some of the major battles fought in this period were the Battle of Charleroi and the Battle of Mons. As a direct consequence of the Battle of the Frontiers, Paris itself came under threat. This happened when the French Fifth Army, which previously managed to delay German movements, became almost completely annihilated by the German 1st and 2nd armies. Both French and the British then commenced a full retreat, and were pursued. In the meanwhile, the French forces from the east managed to reach Paris and mount a defense of the capital. This resulted in the First Battle of the Marne.

At the Marne, the Germans managed to reach positions 70 kilometers outside of Paris. When the British and the French were encountered, the resulting battle became a decisive engagement to dictate the fate of France. It lasted for 6 days, and ended in a full German retreat, ending their plans of conquering France. What happened next was crucial in the development of the Great War: the Germans retreated north across the River Aisne – and there dug in. This established the earliest outlines of the static trench-oriented frontline that would come to define the Western Front. Another attempt was made by the Germans to break the Allied forces and penetrate into France, resulting in the First Battle of Ypres, which ended in a stalemate and finally made it clear that their original plan was simply not going to work.

4.2 – The Brutality of War

The First Battle of Ypres was a costly affair for both the Germans and the Allies, and clearly showcased the direction in which this war was heading. On October 16th began a general move towards the north of Ypres by the British 5th Corps and the French Cavalry divisions. But before progress was made, they confronted three Corps of the German 4th Army on October 18th. After heavy fighting over several days, the Allied defenses around Ypres were reduced a tiny fragment at the outskirts of the city. A decisive result could not be reached on either side, and the casualties kept mounting. It was at the height of this crisis that the key event that would shape the Western Front occurred. Seeing that there is no adequate solution to the stalemate, and that further withdrawal was simply not possible, the Allied forces had the Belgians open the numerous *sluice gates* of the sea, which resulted in the flooding of a huge area of low-lying land. The flooding of the huge area east of the Yser River caused the complete cessation of all combat activities by mid November.

This battle was one of the costlier in the early stages of the war. The French had as much as 85,000 casualties after this battle, while the British had 58,000. The Belgian army was literally halved, suffering more than 20,000 losses. The Germans on the other hand, suffered 130,000 casualties, which clearly show us just how destructive and demanding can attrition warfare be.

One particular event showcased the brutality of this new war and just how different it is than the conflicts of the past. It was the true clash of the traditional and the modern, the first noticeable difference between generations. This event is related to the German university and college students. When the war began, close to 35,000 of these young students promptly volunteered to serve their country. They received only eight weeks of training, and almost all of it focused on the aged methods from past wars. When the Battle of Ypres was well underway, these fresh recruits formed the large part of reinforced 4th Army. They were engaged on October 10th in support of the 6th Army, and then at Langemarck on November 10th. Both of these engagements were catastrophic for the young students. The casualties they suffered were utterly horrific, and amongst the worst that the Germans experienced. This loss of young lives was known as *Kindermord* (Child Death/ Innocents Massacre), with one popular expression ascribed to it: *"These men were to young, and their officers too old".* When the aged methods and tactics of venerable senior officers failed against the new and modern methods of warfare, the youth suffered.

The Western Front became the "iconic" representation of the First World War. The stalemate that ensued after those initial battles dictated the shape of the front between the Entente and the Central Powers, a frontier that won't significantly change for the duration of the war. Those initial battles clearly determined that the warfare of the 20th century is changed for good – old strategies of the 19th century wars simply had no efficiency anymore. This clash between the new and the old resulted in the emergence of *attrition warfare*. The focus shifted towards mass use of artillery, machine guns, and new military industries in order to wear an enemy out and established supremacy on the ground and in the air. As a response to this, trench warfare emerged as the only efficient means of countering the artillery and protecting the infantry. Thus it was that the huge parts of the western fronts were covered with elaborate networks of trenches, between which were huge expanses of *no man's land*. This warfare was especially costly in manpower. Relying on mass charges of the previous wars, officers sent thousands of men in blind charges or slow marches across this no man's land, where they would be easy pickings for new and advanced machine guns or long range artillery.

All of these aspects of the new warfare significantly shaped the western front, which quickly deteriorated into inhumane and near-impossible conditions. Constant artillery barrages from both sides literally obliterated enormous swaths of land, creating a vast and incomprehensible landscape of mud, barbed wire, and craters. Entire villages were wiped away from existence, and the countryside was reshaped. Soldiers and their commanders constantly had to adapt their tactics, developing new weapons and methods on-the-go. Combat was most often reduced to ineffective and catastrophic charges, hand to hand combat, or simply sitting in the muddy trenches and suffering the constant shelling. *This* was war o the worst kind.

The Winter Campaigns of 1914-1915 on the Western Front were particularly costly and exemplified the "pointlessness" of attrition warfare. In the Artois region, combat was done in horrendous weather conditions and in impassable thick mud. Combat was centered on the capture of few ruined villages, which repeatedly changed hands and caused thousands of casualties without a result. The new French offensive in Champagne in January was largely ineffective and stopped due to the same appalling conditions. It was resumed in February, and by March 17th, the French forces managed to capture a forward German position close to the infamous Hill 180. This offensive cost them 240,000 casualties. It was a strategic failure.

Further failures occurred in the Autumn offensives of 1915. The Allied powers once more attempted to make a breakthrough, spending great resources preparing for it. That summer was spent in preparations, with a big focus on aerial reconnaissance to determine German positions. With this help from air photography – another pioneering tactic – the French conducted a more precise bombardment of the German trenches. The consequent attack of the French became the *Third Battle of Artois.* The assault on German trenches began on September 25th, and was difficult for both sides. The attacking French had to face numerous defenses and machine gun emplacements. They were initially successful, but later kept in check by heavily dug in Germans.

Around the same time, the British forces began their offensive, known as the *Battle of Loos*, which eventually became a part of the French engagement. Before attacking the positions, the British wanted to "prepare the ground". This they did by launching a truly devastating artillery barrage of more than 250,000 fired rounds. Even so, their attack failed. Both the British and the French suffered catastrophic casualties and made little to no progress. The effective combination of the trenches and the machine guns was clearly displayed here. The casualties numbered tens of thousands.

4.3 – Attrition Ascended: The Battle of Verdun

By 1916, it became obvious that breakthroughs are a distant and somewhat unreachable objective. The Germans were the first to realize this, seeing their past experiences in 1914. By realizing the new consequences of modern warfare, the Germans opted for a new tactic – mass death. Yes, you read that right. The German command wanted to defeat France by sheer amount of inflicted casualties. Their plan was to limit the Allied provisions by targeting their supply lines, and then to focus on the French positions from which retreat was difficult. One such position they had in mind was the town of *Verdun*, which lay near the frontlines and was strategically closed off. This was the idea of General Erich Von Falkenhayn, the Chief of German General Staff. He focused all his attention on Verdun, establishing air superiority to eliminate threat from above, and conducting devastating artillery barrages. What resulted was the infamous and widely known *Battle of Verdun*. In an attempt to weaken the defenders, Falkenhayn conducted eight hours of full artillery bombardment. The city itself was characterized by a series of ridges and fortifications that surrounded it, and the German command knew that those would be the crucial objectives to take in order to win at Verdun. The battle began on February 21st 1916, and initial fighting was marked by rapid German advance. By the 28th they captured the first key fortification and were halted by French reinforcements.

The next serious conflict was on the famed *Dead Man's Hill* (Le Mort Homme). This height was a key strategic objective for the Germans – it defended the French artillery emplacements. Capturing it meant a key strategic victory against the French. This meant that some of the worst and chaotic fighting of the war was led right here.

The battles for the Dead Man's Hill were devastating. The French artillery dominated the positions, inflicting heavy casualties. The Germans would manage to capture forward French trenches, but bombardment and counter attacks would drive them off. This back and forth fighting lasted for more than a month, and the whole landscape was soon transformed into a mush of craters, blood, and nothingness. It was one of the costliest engagements of the whole year. The Germans eventually captured the hill in late May 1916.

But over that summer, with the change in the French high command, the latter went on an offensive. Step by step, suffering heavy losses, the French managed to repulse the Germans with the aid of artillery, and eventually come out as winners of the Battle of the Verdun. It became known as the *"Mincing Machine"*, and one of the most infamous engagements of the whole war. Close to 355,000 casualties were suffered by the French, and 400,000 by the Germans.

As the losses of Verdun came as a great challenge for the French, the Allied High Command made an attempt to alleviate them, and planned a new offensive that would mainly utilize the British forces. The plan for the offensive was to attack in multiple points around the River Somme, removing the pressure from the French positions and penetrating into German lines. Thus began the Battle of the Somme, on 1st July 1916, when the British divisions, supported by minor French forces, attacked German trenches after several days of heavy rain. The heavy bombardment of the Germans by the British artillery was largely ineffective, and thus the British unknowingly marched towards readied and largely unaffected Germans. During that initial British attack, where the soldiers blindly marched and charged across the muddy ground, the casualties were dazzlingly high. The British suffered 57,000 casualties in a *single day*, the highest amount in the history of the British Army.

Somme was somewhat of a testing ground in itself. Trying to find a lesson in the Verdun battle, the British command attempted to change their approach. The battle thus became prolonged, and the British aimed for air superiority over the Somme battlefield. In July and August, the attacks of the British continued, again with little to no success. In the very final stages of the battle, the British utilized even more divisions, and introduced tanks into the battle

– for the first time ever. Neither worked. By early November 1916, the Battle of the Somme was over, and inconclusive. The British managed to gain just 8 kilometers of ground, driving a bulge into the German salient, but nothing more than this. Thus, it can be argued that the battle was either inconclusive, or an Allied defeat. Either way, it came with a catastrophically high cost of life. The British suffered a mind-numbing 420,000 casualties, while the French suffered 200,000. The Germans most likely had roughly 460,000 casualties. This was one of the bloodiest battles of the Great War.

1917 saw the increased offensives of the Allies, most of which would have a significant outcome on the situation on the Western Front. It was the year of the Flanders Offensive, which began in June. Its goal was to once again remove the mounting pressures on the French army. Ypres once again became the center of fighting with the British attack on the Messines Ridge on June 7th. This battle became notorious for the effective use of mines. This was done by the British Royal Engineer tunnelers, who had been digging under the enemy lines since 1915. They dug deep beneath the ridge and the German positions, and placed approximately 500 tones of high explosives contained in 21 mines. On the day of the British attack in 1917, these mines were detonated, causing enormous devastation. They killed 7,000 German soldiers, and left incomprehensibly large craters. These craters can be observed today, many of which became ponds and lakes. Following the explosions, the British managed to capture the ridge in a single day.

The offensive culminated with the far more devastating *Third Battle of Ypres,* which consisted of *The First and Second Battles of Passchendaele.* Passchendaele was a battle defined by its striking visual aspect: it was conducted in the autumn months after heavy rain. The resulting landscapes were simply a mush of gooey mud and endless bomb craters, with not much in between. This offensive claimed many lives on both sides, both of which were affected by the constant wet weather. It was characterized by almost futile combat – neither side gained much, and the inhumane conditions led to high loss of life. Both sides combined lost more than 500,000 men.

The Western Front was perhaps the bloodiest theater in the Great War. The constant stalemate and the emphasis on attrition warfare placed a high strain on the men on the ground – the true victims of this bloody conflict. The allies had roughly 2,041,000 dead soldiers, of which 1,300,000 were French men. The Central powers on the other hand, had significantly less dead – 1,495,000. Either way, such mindless loss of life is difficult to comprehend by us, everyday readers in the comfort of our homes, a century later. These were the sufferings of our great-grandfathers, men who were the very last of a dying breed. A dying breed whose disappearance was hastened by this ruthless war. It was Europe's finest which laid willingly their lives in the mud and rain of the fields of Flanders, and to them we owe a debt of gratitude. And still we have to ask: Why? How can so much death bring about peace?

And lastly, dare we even imagine how it was for the young and weary men that rushed forth across those battle-scarred muddy landscapes, facing certain death – not even knowing why? Their dreams and hopes, the passionate loves they left behind, the combined ferocity of their desire to live, live, live – all gone in seconds, left to seep into the mud of the no man's land. We are not worthy of such sacrifice.

"Two minutes' silence for the dead.
I thought of the fields when the fields were red.
Red, not with poppies but with blood,
The blood of men, the image of God.
Two minutes' silence for the dead.
Stood in the crowd and bowed my head,
Not in reverence but in shame,
At the insult in memory of their name.
Two minutes' silence for the dead.
Last Post is sounding, eyes are red.
But Reveille is sounding for me instead,
Of the Last Post in Memory of the dead."
Robert Irvine

CHAPTER V
INTO THE
MOUNTAINS: THE
ITALIAN FRONT

WHEN ITALY ENTERED the Great War in 1915, it did so relying on the promises made by the Allied Powers. It had pretensions on several regions under Austro-Hungarian possession, chiefly north Dalmatia, Southern Tyrol, and the Austrian Littoral. From the get-go, the Italian Army hoped to utilize the element of surprise and quickly deal with their objectives against Austria-Hungary. However, the terrain soon put a stop to these ideas: the war in the Alps was a whole new challenge altogether. Instead of the imagined offensives, Italy and its enemy were left with a debilitating war of attrition, much like the one on the Western Front. Trench warfare dominated this theater as well, but there was no mud and rain – instead there was wind and snow. During this front, both the Italian *Alpini* troops, and the German *Gebirgsjäger* were extensively used, as both were specially trained to fight in mountain terrains.

Immediately in 1915, the front got heated, as battles quickly erupted. The opening Italian offensive was aimed at the *Isonzo* River, across which lay the crucial Austrian fortress city of *Gorizia*. What resulted from this offensive is a set of conflicts known as the Battles of Isonzo. The First Battle of Isonzo began on June 23rd 1915, and saw the numerically superior Italians making an attempt at strong Austro-Hungarian fortifications. They failed.

Two weeks later, they tried again. The Second Battle of Isonzo was even fiercer than the first one, and caused high casualties for both sides. It ended in a stalemate.

But, third time's the charm, right? The Italian forces thought so, as they launched the *Third* Battle of Isonzo in October 1915, this time angrier, better armed, and better prepared. They failed. Again. The Austrian defenders repulsed the attack once more.

Once more? The Italians renewed the offensive just six days later, starting the *Fourth* Battle of Isonzo. Can you guess its outcome? The battle ended less than a month later, but not before both sides suffered heavy casualties, and the ammo was exhausted on both sides. There was still no victory. But not to worry – he who dares, wins! Right? The *Fifth* Battle of Isonzo was fought in March 1916, and was again not a success. You won't be surprised to learn that there were *eleven* Battles of Isonzo in total. Gorizia was captured by the Italians in the end, but the price was extremely high.

One of the defining conflicts on the Italian Front, and one that brought its end, was the Battle of Vittorio Veneto, fought from October 24th to November 4th 1918. It was one of the defining achievements of the Italian Army, and the final straw for the already weakened Austro-Hungarian army. The offensive also began at the same time when the ruling Austro-Hungarian Habsburg Monarchy began collapsing, adding to its importance overall.

The Italian Marshal, the chief of staff Armando Diaz decided to act against the Austro-Hungarians after increasing political pressures: he commanded a major offensive that was directed across the River Piave and the strongly fortified positions at Mount Grappa. However, the flooding river prevented the Italian troops from achieving early success – the Austrians managed to resist. However, the flooding soon dropped off, and allowed Italian troops to make progress in the second part of the offensive. After crossing the Piave, and fighting fiercely for three days, the Italians managed to crack the Austro-Hungarian defenses. All of this was happening concurrently with the widespread collapse of the Central Powers in Europe, and that further demoralized the Austrians. Without sufficient ammunition, resources, and manpower, their army was in shambles. The Italians managed to capture tens of thousands of their soldiers, while others simply fled en-masse. The sheer amount of prisoners became a burden on the Italian progress, but it was not to matter – the armistice was soon signed. The Battle of Vittorio Veneto was the most decisive of the Italian Front, but a difficult one nonetheless. It was the last stand of the Austro-Hungarians. The casualties were high: roughly 40,000 for the Italians, and 528,000 for their enemies.

The events of the Italian Front were largely responsible for outcome of the later Italian Unification, which helped establish the Kingdom of Italy. And even though the Italian casualties were high, and the strain of war was demanding, the end result helped place Italy on a stable path. New territories were taken from the dissolved Austria-Hungary, and the role of Italy as a vital Allied power was cemented.

CHAPTER VI
THE WAR OF
MOVEMENTS:
EASTERN FRONT

6.1 – The Slumbering Bear Awakens

NOTICEABLY DIFFERENT from the Western theater was the so-called Eastern Front. Due to the differences in geography, borders, and the parties involved, the Eastern Front was a markedly different experience than the trench warfare of the West. For the most part, the Eastern front stretch from the coast of Baltic in the north, all the way to the Black Sea in the south, with significant parts in the Central Europe as well. It involved the Allied powers on one side – the Russians and the Romanians, with the limited support from France, Britain, and Serbia; and the Central Powers on the other side – the Ottoman Empire, Austria-Hungary, Bulgaria, and Germany.

In the overall historiography of the First World War, the Eastern Front is largely overlooked and misrepresented. Winston Churchill coined the term "unknown war" when referring to it in the post-war years. Still, while the eyes of the world were focused on the devastation in the West, the East was engaged in tragedies and battles of its own. But it was not a war of attrition and stalemate, and mass death, like it was on the Western Front. This was a war of movement and maneuvering, of breakthroughs and new methods of warfare. It was the conflict that pitted two giant empires and their allies against one another: Russia and Austria-Hungary.

At the start of the war, Russia stepped in to support its little cousin Serbia. This decision was driven by the rise of Pan-Slavic sense of awakening, and the Russian Tsar and his people felt an obligation to assist their Slavic brethren. However, it was not all pride and brotherly love: Russia hope to achieve sizeable gains through the conflict, especially on the Black Sea coast which was rich in resources. Moreover, it was bound by alliance to provide assistance to France which was facing the might of Germany. Known as the brooding bear and the giant of Europe, Russia had an army of nearly 3.5 million men upon mobilization. In the north of the Eastern Front, it was facing the German 8th Army in Prussia, and further south were the Austro-Hungarian forces.

The Russian plan of attack was fairly straight forward. This plan was known under the name *"Mobilization Schedule 19"*, through which two Russian Armies consisting of 29 infantry divisions, would be sent to the north in order to invade East Prussia, while the other half of their forces, consisting of four armies of 45 infantry divisions, would shift south and engage the Austro-Hungarians. This was a shrewd and sound tactical approach, with which Russia answered the mounting pressures from the French High Command for their involvement in Prussia, and attempted to quickly defeat the Germans in the East while the latter were focused on the conflict in the West.

Of course, the Austrians and the Germans anticipated these tactics as a possibility, and this resulted in a lot of maneuvering across the front, as both the Russians and the Austrians anticipated the next move of their enemy. Thus it was that the very first conflicts on the Eastern Front occurred on August 23rd, when the Austrian 1st Army, commanded by General Viktor Dankl, met the Russian 4th Army under the command of Baron von Saltza. The battle occurred near the town of *Krasnik*, and was characterized by Austrian frontal charges which repulsed the Russians. They won, but suffered up to 50% losses. Two days later a similar engagement was fought between Austrian 4th Army and the Russian 5th – at Komarow.

The Austrians made an attempt to exploit these victories, but it didn't come to fruition as they shifted further east in response to the looming Russian invasion of Galicia. There they suffered a debilitating defeat at the famous *Battle of Gnila Lipa*. It was led from 26th to 30th August 1914, between the Russian 8th and 3rd armies, commanded by Generals Brusilov and Ruzki, respectively; and the Austro-Hungarian 3rd Army under the command of General Brudermann. The Russian victory was completely decisive – they suffered meager losses compared to several thousand Austrian. The latter's forces were forced into full retreat. General Brusilov's army cashed in on this victory, and managed to capture the L'viv fortress (Lemberg) on September 3rd. This was a part of the wider Battle of Galicia.

This achievement was followed by further Russian success. The Russian Cossack cavalry, which was a highly effective fighting force during the war, discovered a major gap between the positions of Austria's 1st and 4th armies. This gap was a crucial strategic advantage and was quickly exploited by the Russians. The commander of Russia's Southwestern Front, General Ivanov, sent his 5th and 9th armies through this gap and engaged the Austrians in the Battle of Rawa-Ruska on September 3rd. Once more they utterly defeated the Austro-Hungarians, inflicting 60,000 casualties. From there they proceeded to the Austrian stronghold of Przemyśl, to which they laid siege. This siege would last for 133 days, ending in a crushing and humiliating defeat for the Austrians.

6.2 – The Tables Turn

After these Russian successes in the southwest and Galicia, the Austro-Hungarian army was left in shambles. Suffering more than 300,000 casualties – one third of its forces – it could never effectively recover. However, the Russians didn't fare so well in the

North as they did in the South. Faced with the aggressive tactics of the Germans in East Prussia, the Russians quickly got the taste of major defeat.

The Russian Northwestern Front was under the command of General Zhilinsky. He commanded two armies, each with 15 infantry divisions, and ordered an attack against the German 8th army under the command of General von Prittwitz.

To achieve this attack, he opted for a two pronged attack: the Russian 1st army was to focus on the city of Königsberg in the north, while the 2nd army under the command of General Samsonov, was to pass the Masurian lakes and trap the forces of Prittwitz from that side.

But here was a crucial mistake. Zhilinsky separated his force into two armies, and soon enough, they were unable to coordinate their attacks and communicate efficiently. The Germans however, didn't sit idly: General Prittwitz benefited from their lack of coordination. With a combination of aerial reconnaissance and interception of Russian communications, he knew exactly where they were. Nevertheless, the Russians had a crucial advantage in numbers, and managed to defeat Prittwitz with their 1st Army, forcing him to retreat.

The German High Command was not happy with these events, and quickly replaced Prittwitz with the more able General von Hindenburg. The Germans then quickly rebounded and devised a cunning plan with which to fool the Russian 1st army, and focus their forces on the 2nd.

The following engagement lasted between 26th and 30th August, and was known as the Battle of Tannenberg. It was one of the most devastating defeats for the Russians in the Great War. The Germans managed to complete surround Samsonov's 2nd Army, and utterly destroy it. Its last remaining shambles retreated in disarray, and General Samsonov himself, unable to comprehend the magnitude of defeat he experienced, committed suicide the next day. He lost 125,000 men in that battle, compared to no more than 15,000 on the German side.

What occurred next was the crowning achievement of German

forces in East Prussia, and one of the first precursors to the famed *Blitzkrieg* tactics of the Second World War. Relying on the advanced railroad network and good intelligence, the Germans were able to rapidly transfer their forces to the north, in order to face the remaining Russian 1st army. This became known as the *Tannenberg Maneuver*. The ensuing battle, known as the *First Battle of the Masurian Lakes*, was a partial and costly victory for the Germans, but a victory nonetheless. By forcing the Russians into a full retreat, they ejected them from Prussia and back into Russia. They did suffer a lot of casualties: 70,000 compared to Russian 100,000 men. But it was the price they had to pay: this victory saved the Austro-Hungarian forces from collapse in the south, and stabilized the Eastern Front.

The following year, 1915, saw the complete reversal of roles. Now it was time for the Germans and Austro-Hungarians to begin an advance. The German high command came to the conclusion that their main efforts were to be shifted to the East, with many reinforcements being sent to fill the ranks. With the aim of eliminating Russia from the war, they began a major offensive in Spring 1915, known as the Gorlice–Tarnów Offensive. It was a further attempt at driving back the Russians and removing their maintained pressure on the weakened Austro-Hungarian forces in the South. What initially began as a small offensive, turned out into the largest military operation of Germany in 1915, ending in a decisive achievement on the Eastern Front.

Some of the fiercest fighting of this offensive was centered on the high passes of the Carpathian Mountains. For the Russians, these passes were a pathway into the Hungarian plain, and a major threat for Austria-Hungary. Thus the Austrian forces under the command of Conrad von Hötzendorf focused heavily on this region. Both sides suffered from the appalling conditions and heavy casualties, and soon the Austro-Hungarian army was nearly halved. General Conrad had to devise a daring plan in order to relieve his forces from the situation and drive the Russians into retreat at the same time. This he planned to do by joining up with the German forces under General Falkenhayn, and swinging far to the south, hitting the Russian left flank at the Gorlice–Tarnów front.

The German army that was to engage in this attack was the 11th Army, whose command was given over to the experienced and formidable Field Marshal August von Mackensen. Upon learning that the enemy has converged on their flank, the Russian Supreme Commander opted to wait and defend, rather than make counter-moves. Thus the battle began on May 1st 1915, with the Germans and Austrians basing the bulk of their initial attack on devastating and high caliber artillery fire. This was done mostly with their enormous mortars, whose ravaging firepower was used the previous year in devastating French fortifications. Thanks to the shrewd leadership of Mackensen, who made sure to establish aerial supremacy and its superior reconnaissance, the Germans had continual upper hand. Their high caliber field guns were for the most part superior to those of the Russians, and this allowed them to suppress both the enemy guns and their attempts at counter attacking with infantry.

The enormous siege mortars were the special advantage of the Germans. Their shells had so much devastating potential – a single shell left huge craters and decimated numerous men around it. So, after crippling barrages and the decimation of Russian fortifications, the Germans swept in with repeated infantry attacks. The Russian forces eventually broke after suffering huge casualties, and began an all-out retreat. They suffered more than 350,000 casualties – compared to only 87,000 on the enemy side.

This defeat was the start of the so-called *Great Retreat of 1915*, in which the Russian frontlines collapsed, and were abandoned. All Russian armies retreated far back into Russia – moving over 300 miles (~480 km) to the East. This was a strategic decision by the Russian High Command, preventing encirclement and shortening the front.

Nevertheless, 1916 was a year of changes for all sides. The continued difficulties on the Western Front called for an urgent change in the East. For the Allies, it was an imperative that the

Russians engage in a series of tactical offensives, through which the German forces would be shifted eastwards, removing some of the pressure on the British and the French. After the events of 1915 and the retreat of the Russians, the German and Austrian commands could focus their attention elsewhere: Conrad von Hötzendorf turned to the conflict with Italy, while Falkenhayn refocused on the West.

But the Russians were still in the fight. Although they suffered mind boggling casualties in the previous year, and lost the territories previously gained, they were still far from removed from the war. As they were greatly hampered by a general lack of supplies in the 1915, they now set about replenishing them, under the new command of Alexey Polivanov. The new strategy relied on a greater involvement of the public. Many other changes were implemented, a great part of them mimicking those of the Western Allies. Communications were improved, training as well, and more non-commissioned officers were recruited. Russia was getting back to its feet.

6.3 – Brusilov Steps Up

The call of the Allies was certainly heard, but when the Italians asked the same thing of the Russians – to engage the Germans in Galicia in order to relieve pressure from their flanks – virtually every single Russian commander *declined*. The sole exception was General Aleksei Brusilov. What he proposed was a daring plan: He would launch a major offensive on the Southwestern portion of the front, along the 300 miles he commanded over.

What ensued was one of the greatest Russian military achievements of the Great War, later known as the *Brusilov Offensive*. It lasted from May 4th 1916 to late September of that same year, and was centered on the region of present-day western Ukraine – chiefly near the towns of Lemberg (L'viv), Lutsk, and Kovel. It was Brusilov's crowning and greatest achievement.

The success of this offensive lay in Brusilov's new offensive tactics – which were previously not utilized on the Eastern Front. He relied on the experiences gathered from the Allies in the West, and thus prepared for attacking the Austro-Hungarian positions by gathering virtually all of his reserves and creating a network of trenches , ramparts for aerial obstruction, holding areas, and also accomplished sapping to as close as sixty meters away from Austrian positions. Furthermore, he prepared his soldiers and their commanders with extensive reconnaissance photos and well developed plans of attack. One of the unique points of Brusilov's plan was the creation of false trenches – literally painted on the ground – as well as the construction of false wooden artillery emplacements, all with the intent of fooling Austrian air observations. Although aware of the Russian activities – to an extent – and realizing an attack was imminent, the Austrians still believed their positions are impregnable.

Brusilov Offensive began with highly accurate and focused artillery barrages which took the Austrians *completely* by surprise. After creating several breaches along the frontline, the Russian infantry then commenced their attack. The Austrian 4th Army and the Südarmee both held their positions near Lutsk and Brody, where Russian effectiveness was minimal. However, at the frontlines near the town of Sapanow, the Russian effect was utterly devastating. The artillery was devastating on the Austrian positions, and numerous pockets of infantry were kept continuously pinned down. With combined waves of infantry, cavalry, and armored vehicles, the Russians penetrated deep through the created gap – with great success. This was not the only such breach: several successes occurred along the front, and this quickly gave rise to panic in the Austro-Hungarian high command. With constant high speed advances, the Russians were highly successful in their offensive. By the end, they managed to achieve their original goal and divert the Central Powers from the Western Front. They also inflicted devastating casualties on the Austrians, which essentially "broke the back" of the Austro-Hungarian Army. However, all of these successes came at a high price: the casualties were sky high. For Russians, they numbered around 1,000,000 dead and wounded, while for the Central Powers, this number reached close to 1,337,000 men. Up to this day, the Brusilov Offensive is considered to be one of the most lethal offensives in modern military history.

The Eastern Front of the Great War largely petered out in 1917: its importance lay simply in its existence, as the forces of the Central Powers were kept divided as long as it was there. However, Russia was increasingly hampered by its deteriorating internal affairs. The rise of the Bolsheviks and the continual crisis was a significant change in its history. Led by Vladimir Lenin and a cadre of others, took over power in Russia on November 1st 1917, greatly changing the future of the war on the East. Promptly after their rise to power, Russia descended into a brutal Civil War, which would rage on for three years. It was followed by many conflicts, and countless death. The Eastern Front ceased to exist after the Treaty of Brest-Litovsk in 1918, allowing the Central Powers to shift their full attention on the Western Front.

But it was the Eastern Front that formed another major facet of the First World War. It defined the mentality of the Slavic Russian people, and their selfless sacrifices in the battles of this great conflict. Sheer numbers were their advantage – one that their Generals eagerly exploited, often at a too high cost of human life. Similar tactics would be repeated in the Second World War, in which the suffering of this nation reached all new heights. So let it not be forgotten how bravely lives were laid down on all sides: both friend and foe fought bitterly to the very end. Sadly, all this fighting, this whirlwind of war and hate – it engulfed the civilians across the Eastern and Central Europe. It is their sacrifices too that cannot be forgotten.

CHAPTER VII
PIONEERING
TECHNOLOGIES
OF WAR

WITH THE RISE OF INDUSTRIALISM in the decades before the onset of war, mass production became an all too real advantage for all nations involved. This provided a real shift towards a highly modernized approach to warfare for the era, and the rise of many new and advanced technologies. Military technology saw some of the biggest changes during the Great War, and change the nature of warfare forever. While such changes became visible on a smaller scale just a few decades before in the American Civil War, they were all in their infancy back then. It was the First World War that really pioneered the use of machine guns, hand grenades, high caliber artillery, tanks, armored vehicles, warplanes, poison gas, snipers, submarines, and many other new weapons.

But not all of them were a success, and the Great War proved to be one giant test bed for new technologies. Many of them would not be accepted, and all of them further refined in the decades that followed. The partial effectiveness can be contributed mostly to the somewhat fresh shift from the traditional methods of warfare that were established in the 18th and 19th centuries, and the new 20th century technology and industry.

One of the cruelest military technologies that were conceived during the Great War was the use of chemical weapons. It was the first time ever that poison chemicals were used systematically to defeat enemies. Use of poison gasses in warfare was essentially banned even before the onset of the Great War with the Hague Conventions of both 1899 and 1907, as such warfare was considered inhuman, cruel, and dishonorable. But since Germany boasted one of the most advanced chemical industries of the world, with more than 80% of total global chemical production, they eventually resorted to use of poison gas, even if it was banned. Germans believed that this weapon would give them a crucial advantage in the prolonged attrition warfare in the trenches, and become the decisive factor for their victory.

Chemical weapons that were used in the First World War were the infamous mustard gas, chlorine, phosgene, chlorarsine, and tear gas. When it was first used in April of 1915 at the Second Battle of Ypres, chlorine gas was something not before experienced by allied soldiers. This was the first combat test for the Germans, and the success of this cruel weapon was moderate. The Allied soldiers thought that the gas was just a smoke screen, and they advanced into it. The effects were catastrophic: Just around 5:00 pm, the German 4th Army released an incredible 171 tones of chlorine gas across 6.5 kilometers (4 miles) of front line. The French troops engaged suffered 3,000 casualties, of which more than half were fatalities. One combat report can tell us just how nightmarish such a weapon could be:

"...haggard, their overcoats thrown off or opened wide,
their scarves pulled off, running like madmen, directionless,
shouting for water, spitting blood, some even rolling on
the ground making desperate efforts to breathe."

But poison gas was a double edged sword for the Germans. When the wind suddenly changed direction and brought the gas back, they too got a taste of its potency. They suffered moderate casualties as a result, and realized that a more efficient method of gas deployment need to be devised. Nonetheless, they saw firsthand just how potent such a weapon can be. Later on, with the switch to mustard gas, the Allies too began using this weapon. Soldiers on the frontlines had to adapt in any way they could to combat the poisonous winds – the earliest methods were rags soaked in water or urine, through which the gas could not be inhaled. Afterwards, the technology once more adapted, with the rise of elaborate gas masks. It is widely agreed that use of gas in the Great War has caused more than a million casualties, showing us just how severe the use of chemical weapons can be. And not only is it a truly cruel way for a man to perish, it is also a highly efficient psychological weapon, aimed at putting fear into any man.

7.1 – The Rise of Flight

One of the most famous novelties of the early 20th century, and the Great War, was without a doubt *aviation.* It became one of the most efficient, reliable, and iconic new technologies of the war, and progressed extremely rapidly through the course of the conflict. Commercial aviation and the so-called Rise of Flight were soon militarized, and air combat became a reality in no time. Dashing fighter aces on both sides were a big influence on the morale of the soldiers on the ground, but it was not the only value of aviation – reconnaissance, aerial bombardment, artillery spotting, and overall aerial supremacy quickly became crucial advantages in the war.

In the early stages of the war, aviation had a noticeably primitive character, and was received with much skepticism. But when its efficiency was realized, the industry received quite a push, and novelties were quick to follow.

One of the first uses of airplanes for military purposes occurred at the very start of the war, on the Serbian front. Miodrag Tomić (Миодраг Томић), a Serbian pilot flying in his crude Blériot XI plane was engaged in the first ever dogfight: While on a mission, he came upon an Austro-Hungarian plane. The two pilots then exchanged pistol fire, without success. This occurrence has proven that airplanes will inevitably fight one another, and from that point on, arming them became a priority for all nations involved. From this point on, aviation really became the focus and the leading developing technology of the war. Major powers fought to create better armed and more maneuverable airplanes, hoping to gain a crucial advantage in the air.

When early aviation is considered, there was a major obstacle that designers struggled to overcome. That obstacle was *firepower.* Aviation factories fought to find an adequate solution that would allow single seater airplanes to be equipped with machine guns in order to attain aerial supremacy. After the earliest dogfights on the Serbian front, their aged Bleriot planes were equipped with top-mounted machine guns. The British and the French followed this concept, and soon enough their planes had forward mounted machine guns. A great example is the De Havilland Airco D.H.2, an early airplane of the allies, with a rear mounted engine. This solution was reached because the allies lacked the ability to synchronize the machine gun fire and the rotation of the propeller blades. The Germans gained a significant advantage by being the first to master this obstacle. This was done by developing the so-called *synchronization gear*, a device that allowed a machine gun to be fired *through* the spinning propeller blades, without hitting them.

With this highly advanced design, the Germans quickly gained an upper hand in the air. Synchronization was a revolutionary achievement, and the first planes equipped with it were the infamous Fokker Eindecker monoplanes. By late 1915, the period known as the "Fokker Scourge" left the allies completely incapacitated in air, suffering great losses. This was a startling insight in just how effective synchronized firing really is, and how aviation can quickly make a shift in the flow of the war. The Allies struggled to respond to this new threat, and by January 1916, new airplane models were sent to the front. These were the French Nieuport 11, or the British F.E.2b and D.H.2, neither of which possessed synchronization, but still managed to mount forward firing machine guns outside of the arc of the propeller. This stop-gap configuration proved to be an adequate response to the German planes, and the situation in the air became somewhat evened out.

Throughout the war, fighter pilots held an almost legendary status. As air combat became a daily occurrence, and new tactics and strategies were developed regularly, fighter pilots quickly got the opportunity to excel and make a difference through their skill in piloting. Those who scored a certain number of aerial victories became fighter *aces*, gaining fame and reputation, both amongst their comrades and their foes. Easily the most successful and most famous of all fighter pilots of the First World War was none other than the *Red Baron*, Manfred Von Richtofen, the top scoring German ace who is credited with 80 aerial victories. The daring feats of him and his squadrons became a huge morale booster for the troops on the ground, but also gained him much respect from his enemies.

The war in the air remained a focal point of the war until its end, and ushered the world into a new sphere of warfare. Air domination was found out to play a significant role, as it allowed better reconnaissance, swifter attacks, and adequate artillery spotting.

7.2 – The Lumbering Knights: Armored Warfare

As the war progressed, the nations involved moved forward as well – in the technological aspect. One of the great innovations of the First World War is certainly the *tank*. As the debilitating stalemate of the trench warfare on the Western Front began taking an increasing toll on both sides, a new and efficient solution had to be found. Casualties became unbearable on both sides, which was the number one "push" towards the creation of a new weapon. Even before the onset of war, an idea for an all-terrain vehicle was talked about, and now the time came where such a design was more than needed. The British were the first to achieve it, coming forward with prototype "landship" designs. The so-called *Little Willie,* a prototype, was showcased in 1915, followed by the refined design known as the *Mark I.* Soon the name "tank" was used for these vehicles, rather than the obsolete term *landship.*

The main idea of a tank on the Western Front was an ability to cross trenches and eliminate barbed wire obstacles, all the while being able to withstand enemy fire. Add to this the ability to shoot back, and you have a potent fighting machine which can turn the tide of the war. To combine all of these features into a single vehicle, the British opted for great length: the initial Mark I heavy tank was 7.75 meters long (25 ft 5 in), and 9.91 meters long with an attached tail (32 ft 6 in). This allowed crossing of wide trenches. The other feature was the armament: a tank in the "male" configuration boasted two Hotchkiss 6 pounder cannons, and three additional .303 machine guns; while the "female" configuration had five machine guns in total. The Mark I tank was a successful design, and saw several versions – from Mark I to Mark X.

By 1917, the French presented their tank designs as well. Contrary to the British, who boasted a coordinated committee for tank designs, the French relied on several rival companies, competing for the job. This resulted in two early tank models, the cumbersome *St. Chamond* tank, and the unreliable *Schneider CA*, both of them large and slow. It wasn't until the *Renault* company came into the mix that a proper French tank came into service. This was a complete opposite from what was shown up to that point – where all the previous designs were for *heavy* tanks, Renault opted for a *light* tank design. The end result was the Renault FT – a shorter, lighter, more maneuverable 2-man tank with the first fully rotating turret. It proved to be reliable and efficient, although boasting a small caliber gun. This tank entered service in 1917, and over 3,000 of them were made during the war – mostly in 1918. The design was a great success, and it even saw service in the Second World War, in many nations around the world.

And it wasn't just the tanks that presented a big and unorthodox change in ground warfare. The military industry quickly began experimenting with a variety of armed and armored vehicles, which gave rise to the trend of mobile and decently protected armored cars, tracked artillery movers, and a whole host of unique designs – most of which ended up in the history's dust bin. Either way, the one-of-a-kind blend of the traditional viewpoints and the modern rise of industry was a sure way to revolutionize warfare as it was known up to that point. And in the early 20th century, the Great War proved to be the first true testing ground for new methods of warfare that will become established military branches in the decades to follow.

CHAPTER VIII
TRENCH WARFARE
AND THE WAR OF
ATTRITION

THE WESTERN FRONT IN the Great War was certainly marked by a number of technological innovations and pioneering military inventions, but one aspect defined it more than any other. That aspect is trench warfare, and it directly relates to the quickly emerging attrition warfare of that front – marked by stalemates, sieges, and overall grueling warfare of wearing down your opponent. Trench warfare was a direct consequence of newly emerging style of warfare, when new weaponry, tactics, and increase in firepower could not be matched by the largely traditional infantry. In such an environment, the successful defender was at an advantage. Thus, in order to gain the upper hand, enemies relied on elaborate and extensive networks of trenches and dugouts that related to the attrition warfare employed. Trench warfare resulted in severe casualties for each side that attempted to cross the "no man's land" in between trench systems – clearly pointing out to the advantage of the defender in these situations.

In the case of the First World War, trenches became a symbol for the mindlessness of war, and just how devastating it can be when spread out onto a global scale. Coordinated attacks from trenches were marked by futile charges and extremely high casualties, and as such are symbolic of war's futility. In the Great War, "going over the top" was synonymous with certain death: in all great battles of the Western Front, tens of thousands of young men would lose their lives without even getting a chance to fight back or make a significant difference. This was due to the fact that "going over the top" involved a mindless charge across open land, almost always in direct line of fire. Such attacks often ended in disaster – since enemy machine gunners and riflemen had a clear shot of the advancing enemy. The clear example of this is the first day of the Battle of the Somme in 1916, when the British lost 60,000 young men – arguably in vain.

The Great War was certainly a testing ground on an enormous and malicious scale. Each year brought new advancement as enemies adapted to the new tactics and technologies that their opponents presented. In the very first years of the war, trenches became a reliable method of defense – which, as we mentioned, came as an advantage.

A trench system was developed to be an almost continuous and elaborate network – with countless connections between parallel trenches that allowed for an efficient system of communications and resupply. Depending on their depth and complexity, trenches were very efficient as a defense against artillery – being below the surface of the ground and arguably better than above-ground concrete structures. And if we consider that the Great War saw the widespread use of artillery – more than ever before – trenches at the time certainly proved to be a reliable approach.

The 20th century said a fond farewell to the grand battles of old. Gone were the glorious days of Generals such as Napoleon or Bagration: this was the era of industry and attrition. And this meant that heavy bombardment was the key to breaking an enemy. From horseback and rank file, the men shifted towards dirt and mud, and the battle of steel nerves, as only the tougher enemy will come on top in that grueling chaos that is attrition warfare.

Trenches in the Great War came in a few different designs, mostly depending on their importance and strategic position. Those that were more significant had to boast a complex and sturdy design, allowing good enough conditions for the soldiers who had to live there. This meant that a *quality* trench had the depth of at least 8 feet (~2.5 meters), in which men could stand upright without being in direct danger. Furthermore, such important trench lines were almost never simply straight: instead they relied on a tactical method of zig-zag and stepped designs, in which each straight line was only a few meters or yards short. The main advantage of this design was to limit the blast of an artillery shell or a grenade that strikes directly into the trench – the stepped pattern would largely contain the blast. It was also an efficient way to remove the threat of enfilade if the trench was invaded by enemy soldiers. Enfilade is a volley of fire in a straight line – something that posed as a very real threat in straight line trenches.

Better trenches were then lined on the bottom with wood duckboards or raised wooden frames. This allowed the soldiers to have a firmer grip while travelling the trench, and also kept the rainwater and mud below. The side walls of a trench would be also lined – most often with walls of sand bags and with wood frames or thin iron sheets. Throughout the war, trenches varied from combatant to combatant, and from area to area. While the British and French oft relied on proven construction methods and established dimensions, the Germans often took it a step further. Their trenches were often deeper – usually around 4 meters (12 feet) – and could contain special dug-in rooms for officers, tunnels, and storage and sleeping rooms that would be dug underground and spread several stories underground.

Trench warfare brought with it an entirely new aspect of soldierly life – one that required adaptation, sacrifice, and fear. A soldier could spend as much as two weeks in a forward, frontline trench, or as little as a single day – before being relieved and send to other tasks. That meant that a trench system needed to accommodate for some humane conditions as much as possible. The time spent in a trench varied from side to side, and from manpower at disposal.

But even with quality construction, life in the trenches was rarely humane or acceptable. For a good part of the year, trenches were hampered by constant mud, water, dampness, and disease. Even with the tactical advantages of a trench defense system, rates of death were still high. The main contributor to this was the almost incessant artillery fire. An incredible 75% of all known casualties in trenches is due to artillery. Those men that were not victims of direct hits, would succumb to devastating shell fragments and shrapnel.

Another key cause of loss of life was disease and poor hygiene in the trenches. The main disease was the so-called Trench Fever, which would emerge from body lice, which was a constant nuisance of all soldiers. Trench fever is a moderately serious illness, but in the Great War, with the medicine still lacking crucial advancements (especially in a frontline trench), it was almost certainly fatal. It caused nausea, rashes, fever, and continual lethargy. Furthermore, the poor conditions meant that any minor infection could be fatal in a trench. Often left untreated, they would fester and prove fatal in many cases. Add to this the inability to properly dispose of the mass casualties, and you are left with a truly grim and unforgiving image of just a single of Great War's numerous ugly facets.

Another thing that the advent of trench warfare brought on is a different approach to combat. Soldiers had to constantly adapt to new conditions, and to come with new and inventive ways to defeat their enemy and gain an upper hand in the cramped and unforgiving conditions of the trenches. First and foremost of these weapons were grenades, whose worth was quickly noticed. So much so, that hand grenades became a preferred weapon of most soldiers. Properly thrown, a grenade could have devastating effects in a narrow trench. Not only did the blast kill or wound several soldiers, but the grenade also made the attacker shielded from enemy fire – you didn't have to expose yourself to throw it. This then saw the rise of unique methods of increasing the distance a grenade could be thrown. Rifle mounted rods for grenade launching, unique crossbow-type launchers, and the iconic "potato masher" German grenades are all typical examples of ingenious designs developed in the era.

But when it came to hand to hand combat, which was the most frightening and culminating point of trench warfare, grenades and rifles often came second place. If a group of soldiers manages to cross no man's land and invade an enemy trench, what usually follows is ferocious close combat. And in such a case you couldn't really use your bolt action rifle with much effect, nor could you throw a grenade so close to yourself and your fellows. For this very reason, soldiers relied on a very primitive aspect of warfare, borrowing designs from medieval periods. These were all sorts of new melee weapons. Most common were *trench clubs*, usually crude and made by company smiths and engineers from whatever parts could be scrounged up. These maces were brutal and highly effective in hand to hand combat, and widely used during the Great War, thanks to their efficiency. Specially designed knives were used also. While bayonets were standard issue and designed for close combat, many soldiers didn't like them because they proved to be unwieldy and prone to getting stuck in a pierced enemy. This gave rise to combat trench knives and brass knuckles, with which you could kill an enemy swiftly and efficiently, continuing combat almost immediately.

Still, in order to actually get to use these primeval melee weapons, soldiers first needed to successfully cross the no man's land. And that was an entire challenge for itself. Because crossing it, soldiers needed to deal with one of the most menacing and troublesome barriers a man can face: *barbed wire.* This simple barrier was extremely effective at stopping advancing enemy infantry, and directly caused numerous casualties on both sides. Also known as razor wire, it would be placed all along the frontlines, and would be very difficult to bypass once in place. A soldier who faced this obstacle was forced to either cut through it, find an opening, or bypass it some other way. Failing to do so would result in certain death: a man quickly got stuck in the jumble of wires, getting exposed to enemy fire and easily targeted. In managing to get unstuck, a man would end up with a number of razor cuts, which could get infected and prove to be lethal soon after. Barbed wire positions were often directly in line of machine gun fire, which would deal with trapped soldiers and inflict heavy losses in the process.

There is little doubt that trench warfare was one of the ugliest and fiercest aspects of the Great War – a nightmarish depiction of how warfare can quickly degrade to inhuman conditions when it becomes stationary and enters the attrition phase. From Somme to Ypres and Passchendaele, all the way to the hilly Dolomites and the Easter Front – trenches were the inescapable aspect of this deadly conflict. And with surety of mute witnesses, we can say that no one would want to be situated in that muddy hell where each minute brings new expectations of a truly grim and frightening end, with death looming at every corner. Trench warfare meant only one certain thing for the common soldier of the First World War: *fear.*

CHAPTER IX
PACIFIC AND ASIA –
THE STRUGGLE FOR
NAVAL DOMINATION

WITH THE ENTRY OF NEW Zealand and Australia into the war, the conflicts soon engulfed Asia and the Pacific, where both the Allies and the Germans had colonial possessions. Although not as devastating as some other theaters of war, it was nonetheless extremely significant and had a big influence on the latter outcome of the war. It lasted from August 3rd 1914, until January 5th 1919. The main focus of the Asian and Pacific theatre was on naval warfare and the supremacy in the water, all the while targeting the colonial possessions of Germany. Many of the engagements during this four and a half period were bloodless, while a few brought with them moderate casualties. Of all the engagements though, the most significant was the Siege of the Chinese port of Tsingtao, then in the German hands.

Due to the nature of the nations and colonies in the Pacific, gaining naval supremacy was the main focus of all parties involved. By controlling major trade routes, blockading ports, and engaging in port sieges, significant advantage can be gained over the enemy.

As mentioned, the Siege of Tsingtao (Qingdao) was the defining engagement in this theatre of war. An important port in the possession of Germany, it had significant strategic importance. German military presence was moderate – numbering close to 4,000 troops centered on extensive fortifications and trenches.

Previously to the siege, Germany was faced with an ultimatum from Japan. It requested prompt withdrawal of German naval forces from the Chinese and Japanese waters, and the abandonment of the Tsingtao port. Japan entered the Great War in 1914 on the side of the Allies, seeking to exploit the unfavorable position of Germany and to expand its influence and territories in Asia. The refusal of that ultimatum meant the inevitable attack on Tsingtao, and the German defenders meant to be prepared for it.

Eager to claim the port and assert their dominance in the region, the Japanese sent almost their entire fleet, of which there were five battleships, two battle cruisers, two destroyers, one airplane carrier, and so on. Furthermore, they sent a contingent of 23,000 soldiers, gaining a significant advantage over the defending Germans. These forces were further bolstered by aid from the British, and the Chinese, both of whom sent several thousand additional troops.

Compared to these overwhelming forces, the German garrison numbered just 3,625 soldiers in total, which was the entirety of Germany's East Asian force. The soldiers were supported by a modest naval force: four light gun boats, a single protected cruiser, and a single torpedo boat. Even though they were outnumbered, the German vessels had moderate successes early on: the S90 torpedo boat managed to inflict heavy damage on HMS Kennet, a British Royal Navy destroyer, while the gunboat *Jaguar* managed to sink the Japanese destroyer Sarotaye. The S90 later on inflicted another heavy loss for the Japanese navy by sneaking out of the harbor and sinking the protected cruiser *Takachiho*, claiming 271 lives.

The Siege of Tsingtao began officially on October 31st, with the first bombardment of the fortifications. The German positions were under constant shelling day and night for seven days, being able only to respond with moderate counter-fire until they ran out of ammunition on November 6th. When this happened, the Japanese soldiers overwhelmed the defenses on the shore by successive waves of attacks. The following day, November 7th, officially ended the Siege of Tsingtao with the surrender of the German commanders. Over 3,500 German soldiers were taken prisoner, while 199 men lost their lives, and 503 were wounded. For the Allied forces, these numbers were somewhat higher: 727 men were killed, and 1,335 wounded. The Siege of Tsingtao was also the place of the first aerial victory in aviation history: the Germans had a single *Taube* airplane in their possession – it was flown successfully during the siege, and its pilot downed a Japanese Farman plane with nothing but his pistol.

9.1 – Gaining the Upper Hand

In the pacific, the developing actions were less costly in manpower. In fact, one of the crucial engagements was actually *bloodless*, a welcome change in the tumultuous conflict that was the Great War. This was the strategically important offensive undertaken by the New Zealand forces aimed at the one of Germany's Pacific colonies, *German Samoa.* A force of more than one thousand New Zealand soldiers was supported by six cruisers of Australian and French navies, as they landed on the islands of Samoa on August 29th 1914. The meager German force showed no resistance – after sabotaging their radio equipment, the islands were occupied without bloodshed.

Things were not so peaceful in *German New Guinea,* another of Germany's overseas colonies. It was attacked in September of 1914 by the Australians. This invasion quickly escalated – on the island of *New Britain*, a force of 500 Australian soldiers engaged in battle against a force of 61 Germans who were bolstered by 240 men of the Melanesian police. This swift battle ended in a decisive Australian victory, with both sides suffering light losses. After this defeat, the German command retreated to Toma outside the port of Rabaul, on New Britain. There, after a short and bloodless siege which lasted from 14th to 17th September 1914, the German command surrendered and the Australians officially occupied the territory of German New Guinea. As the war progressed, further German colonies were claimed by the Allied Powers, including German Micronesia, the Marshall Islands, and others.

When naval forces are considered, the Allies managed to retain significant supremacy thanks to the numerical advantage they had. The Germany's *East Asia Squadron*, an Imperial Navy Cruiser force commanded by Admiral Maximilian von Spee, embarked on a long retreat across the Pacific after the fall of Tsingtao. Their goal was to return to Germany. But they made it their objective to conduct several raids as they withdrew. Of these actions, a significant one was the raid of Fanning Island in the region of Kiribati in the Pacific. An important Allied cable relay station was destroyed in this action. Another important event was the naval bombardment of Papeete, the capital of French Polynesia, in which material losses were high for the town.

But as their retreat got them closer to South America, the East Asia Squadron became engaged in more serious actions. The first of these was the important *Battle of Coronel*, fought just off the coast of Chile on November 1st 1914. Facing a squadron of British cruiser, Admiral von Spee's ships managed to win a crucial victory: two British cruisers were sunk, and more than 1,500 British sailors died. The Germans suffered only 3 wounded men.

But that was the last stroke of luck for the East Asia Squadron. About a month after this victory, they engaged in the *Battle of the Falklands*, in which nearly entire fleet was sunk by the British ships. Admiral Maximilian Von Spee was killed in this engagement – going down with his ship. His two sons also died. Only two ships managed to escape the battle.

While this proved to be the end of the fleet, several of its lone ships – left behind by Admiral Spee before the retreat began – engaged in moderately successful actions, trying to disrupt Allied shipping to the best of their ability.

One of the two ships that fled the Falklands was the light cruiser *Dresden*. Its crew chose to return back to the open waters of the Pacific ocean, hoping to raid Allied shipping. They sailed the Pacific until March 1915, when the engines began giving up.

Attempting to sail back to Chile, *Dresden* encountered a small British Naval contingent, and was scuttled by its crew after a short and desperate battle.

A far more interesting fate was reserved for *SMS Emden*, a light cruiser which Admiral von Spee deliberately left behind as he began his retreat. Emden was commanded by the highly skilled captain, Karl von Müller. Detached from the rest of the East Asia Squadron and acting alone, Emden was first engaged in the successful *Battle of Penang* in October 1914, in which it sank two ships – a French destroyer and a Russian cruiser. Continuing on its solitary path, the vessel engaged in numerous attacks on Allied shipping and merchant vessels, and managed to sink more than 30 of them – a significant achievement. Another crucial action was the naval bombing of the Indian port of Madras, in which key British oil reserves were heavily damaged.

This successfully path of SMS Emden ended in November 1914, after the ship was engaged in the 1-on-1 *Battle of Cocos*, in which it was beached and destroyed by the light cruiser *Sydney* of the Royal Australian Navy, with a large part of its crew killed in action. A part of the survivors, the captain included, were taken prisoner. However, a crew of about 50 men got stranded on the shores of Cocos Island. From there, they commandeered a small schooner, in which they managed to sail 11,000 kilometres (6,800 mi) across the ocean and reach safety – a feat that was achieved just a few times in entire history.

Another unique and adventurous fate was reserved for *SMS Seeadler*, another ship that remained solitary. The Seeadler was one of the last *sailing* ships, meaning that it had three masts and relied on wind for its movement. Commanded by Graf von Luckner, it too had a very successful solo run: although it was a masted sailing ship, it was also a fighting one. It conducted several successful attacks and raids on Allied shipping, and sank numerous vessels. In the course of their run, the crew acquired a number of allied prisoners of war. Together, they got wrecked in August 1917 at an island in French Polynesia, where they were forced to settle. When food became scarce, the German crew departed the island in a lifeboat, abandoning the allied prisoners to their fate. The lifeboat managed to sail across the ocean and reach Fiji, where under the command of Luckner they managed to capture a French schooner ship. This ship too eventually was lost, and the crew interned in Chile.

During the course of the Great War in Asia, China was a continuously torn nation. Even before the outbreak of conflict, foreign influence in its internal affairs caused great issues: the Boxer Rebellion which saw involvement from all major European Powers was a fight from the Chinese rebels to expel the invaders. It failed.

During the 1917, China saw rival factions with opposing views, and a lot of confusion. So it was that the German government was thought to be involved in the so-called *Manchu Restoration* of 1917, a monarchist coup led by Zhang Xun with an aim to return the Emperor Puyi of the Qing Dynasty to the throne. The accusation against the Germans stated that their support of this coup intended to prevent Chinese support to the allies from the pro-war faction under Duan Qirui. The Manchu Restoration eventually failed, and both the accusation and the failure were used as a suitable pretext for China to declare war on Germany.

Around that same time, in 1917, another unlikely nation entered the war by declaring war on both Germany and Austria-Hungary. That nation was *Siam*, nowadays known as Thailand. The war was declared on July 22nd, 1917, and the Siamese at once captured 12 German ships that were docked in its ports. When compared to other Asian and Pacific countries, Siam was never made a colony: it remained independent and entered the war of its own volition, and thus became an equal of other Allied powers. Of course, this declaration of war was a sure way for the Siamese King Rama VI to gain favor and support from the allies – mainly British. This was the clear insight into the foreign policy of Siam and their desire to associate themselves with the major world powers. Siam went as far as to change its flag to contain red, white, and blue – the allied colors.

In 1918, the *Siamese Expeditionary Force* was organized and sent overseas to take part in action on the Western Front. These Siamese troops were involved in both air and ground combat, and took part in the Second Battle of the Marne, and the Meuse-Argonne offensives.

The Asian theatre of war was by far the most adventurous one and the one with least casualties. Nonetheless, it played a huge role in the Great War, with the Allies gaining a clear upper hand right from the start. By placing the German Asian and Pacific colonies under their control, the Allied powers managed to significantly weaken their opponent. Naval warfare was the focus of these campaigns, and it became clear that the next conflict in the waters of the Pacific will require absolute naval domination.

DEFEATING THE LION OF AFRIKA: AFRICAN CAMPAIGNS

10.1 – A Complex Colonial Setup

BEING THE FIRST TRULY *global* war, the First World War was like a wildfire – it spread many corners of the world, and engulfed in war regions far away from Europe. One such theatre of war was the African Theatre, a series of campaigns on the soil of the African continent, which lasted from August 1914 to November 1918. The several campaigns were centered on the North African regions, and were prompted by the Ottoman Empire and the German Empire, both of which had territories there. Moreover, almost all of West European major powers had colonies in Africa, and these quickly became embroiled in the war. Not only were they a source of manpower for fighting the war, but were also the source of rich resources needed to fuel the industries of war. As such, the African continent was an important honey pot for the Empires of Europe, who wanted to exploit its every advantage. It was rich in gold, iron, sugar, silver, cocoa, petroleum, and other crucial imports. And in the few years of competitive tensions before the outbreak of war, gaining and retaining supremacy of these colonies was imperative for Europe's major powers.

In 1914, the German Empire's colonies in Africa were comprised of: German West Africa, i.e. Kamerun, Neukamerun, and Togoland; German East Africa; and German South West Africa. These vast, resource-rich territories were enormous in regards to square mileage, many of them being several times larger than some contemporary European nations. All of these colonies comprised of modern-day African nations like Togo, Burundi, Tanzania, Namibia, Rwanda, and Cameroon, as well as parts of Chad, Mozambique, Nigeria, Congo, Ghana, and so on.

France, on the other hand, had significantly larger colonial territories, almost dwarfing those occupied by Germany. These territories were better known as the *French Colonial Empire,* through which France had overlordship over many nations and regions in Africa, Asia, Caribbean, and Americas. In regards to Africa, this region was incredibly vast: France occupied the Ivory Coast, French Sudan, Dahomey, Senegal, Niger, Mauritania, Upper Volta (Burkina Faso), Guinea, Gabon, Cameroon, and many other regions.

On the other hand, Britain possessed a vast colonial empire that reached far. The most famous territory is the *British Raj*, or the British rule of India, which lasted until 1947. But in regards to Africa, Britain had considerable territories: British West Africa, consisting of Ghana, Gambia, Nigeria, South Cameroon, Sierra Leone, and others. And in the British South Africa, there were Rhodesia, South Africa, Malawi, Botswana, and others. All of these territories meant certain conflict for these European nations, and the quick emergence of the African Theatre would prove that.

One of the very first conflicts to break out on African soil was the North African Zaian War. This conflict broke out nearly seven years after the start of the lengthy French conquest of Morocco. The main opposition during this conquest was the so-called *Zaian Confederation* of various Berber tribes. This opposition quickly escalated into a war with the French. The conflict escalated even further with the news of the Great War: France had to significantly cut their military presence in Morocco, and the Central Powers, Germany especially, sought to capitalize on the situation by aiding the Zaian Confederation in several ways. Even so, the French kept a foothold in Morocco, since the war with the Berbers considered mostly of repeated skirmishes and light raids. The Zaian War continued even after the First World War ended, lasting until 1921 and ending with a decisive French Victory. Nonetheless, the Berber tribes continued a guerilla war against the occupation well into the 1930's.

Placing even more stress on France's colonial rule during their struggle in mainland Europe, the Volta-Bani War came as an unexpected revolt against colonialism. It spread out from revolts in modern day Mali and Burkina Faso, where local indigenous tribes banded together – chiefly the Bobo, Nuni, Bwa, and Lela peoples. What started as a localized uprising, soon spread out into a war, where the tribes mustered considerable force which was spread on several fronts. The war lasted from 1915 to 1917, and gave the French rule in this region several serious setbacks. The rebels organized two suppressive campaigns, both of which were a failure against the modern French colonial army. This war came as a sobering warning for the French, and even though they won, they created the region of Upper Volta as the direct result of this conflict.

But when it comes to direct conflict between European powers, the Togoland Campaign of August 1914, stands out as one of the first such on African soil. This campaign saw the attempt by the French and British forces to invade *Togoland*, a vast colony of the German Empire located in West Africa. The Allies opted for a two-pronged attack, with the French army invading from their colony of Dahomey (known now as Benin), while the British moved in from Gold Coast in the west. Although lasting for only 20 days, the Togoland Campaign had a significant impact on German Colonial rule. Faced with the overwhelming forces of the Allies, the German forces attempted to fight delaying actions while retreating North. After losing several key battles, the Germans were forced out of Togoland and lost the colony, which was later split up by the victors. Losing Togoland was just the first in a series of defeats that led to the eventual loss of German African colonies. One of the battles in the Togoland Campaign claimed the life of Lieutenant George Masterman Thompson, a member of the 1st Battalion Royal Scots of the British Army, who was killed on August 22nd, 1914, while storming German trenches near Chra

Village in Togoland. He was 24, and the first British Officer to lay his life in the First World War.

10.2 – The Lion Keeps Resisting

The war in Africa progressed even further with the onset of the British Kamerun Campaign. This attack was aimed as another attempt to further weaken the German colonial rule in Central and Western Africa. The territory of German *Kamerun* was invaded by a combined Allied force of British, French, and Belgian troops in August 1914, and lasted until 1916, almost full two years. When the entire African theatre is considered, this campaign inflicted significant casualties for both sides, but especially the Germans. Even from the get go, the Germans were both outnumbered and surrounded, since the territory of Kamerun was surrounded on all sides by Allied colonies. The entire campaign was marked by a series of sieges, skirmishes, and full-fledged battles, all being the direct result of Allied advances and offensives.

The most significant of these were the First and Second Battles of Garua, in 1914 and 1915, respectively. Centered on the port city of Garua, the battles were an attempt by the British to defeat the entrenched and fortified Germans. The first battle ended as a thorough success for the Germans, whose positions could not be broken by the British. The latter suffered heavy casualties, losing its full officer core.

The Germans sought to exploit this victory by conducting several offensives into the territory of British Nigeria, much to the dismay of the British command. After these offensives, the British and the French once again focused on the fortifications at Garua, this time seeking to eliminate it for good. But in the meanwhile, the Germans heavily dug-in, creating a system of trenches and forts that could withstand a frontal attack with ease. That is exactly why the British opted for a siege: they created counter-trenches and conducted sapping and mining operations that gradually weakened the defending German garrison. They then opted for naval bombardment of the garrison, which inflicted extreme casualties and prompted the unconditional German surrender in

Garua. After suffering a further series of losses from the Allied armies encroaching from all sides, the German command led by Schutztruppe Commander Carl Heinrich Zimmerman, saw that the Kamerun Campaign was lost. A full retreat was ordered and all German troops that remained were extracted from the region.

On the eastern portion of the African continent, things fared no better. Amongst the most important operations here is the East African Campaign, centered on the Deutsch-Ostafrika region, later spreading like wildfire to neighboring colonies. It was also one of the longest fought on African soil – lasting from 3rd August 1914, all the way to November 25th 1918. Moreover, this campaign was perhaps the most serious engagement in Africa, with very high casualties for all parties involved.

At the time, the German Colonial Forces were headed by Lieutenant Colonel Paul Von Lettow-Vorbeck, better known as the *Lion of Africa* (Der Löwe von Afrika), a commander who would acquire a legendary status for his achievements in Africa in the Great War. His chief objective and the one on which he based his strategy, was to divert the Allied forces and their focus from the Western Front in Europe and onto Africa.

The largest portion of all German troops in Africa was situated in the East, but even so they were greatly outnumbered by the combined troops of the Allies. The intention of Von Lettow was to force the Allies into invading Deutsch-Ostafrika, and thus allow him to fight a defensive war. The German positions also threatened the Ugandan Railway, which was an important asset for the British. They also posed a great threat for the neighboring Belgian colony of Congo.

The conflict in East Africa began in earnest on August 5th 1914, when British forces of the Uganda Protectorate attacked German positions on Lake Victoria. The opening stages of the campaign were troubled by great confusion on both sides. Three days later, British navy cruisers bombarded German wireless station at Dar-es-Salaam. Von Lettow then focused his attention on defending a key strategic port city of Tanga, which the British intended to assault from the water. This resulted in the *Battle of Tanga*.

Von Lettow and his German troops were outnumbered 8 to 1, an enormous disadvantage. But even so, the defenders under the command of the *Lion of Afrika* managed to repulse the British attackers and to gain a decisive and complete victory.

At the very same time, the *Battle of Kilimanjaro* was underway. Running parallel to the Battle of Tanga, it was a plan by the Brigadier-General Aitken, to invade and sieze German East Africa in a swift and decisive offensive. Here to, the German forces were outnumbered, this time 4 to 1. And yet again, they completely defeated the British forces. In the wake of these two victories, Von Lettow's troops gained significant supplies, weapons, and ammo from the retreating British troops.

Thus it was that the "Löwe von Afrika", Paul Von Lettow-Vorbeck, managed to repulse and fight the Allied armies of 300,000 men, with his outnumbered contingent of just 14,000 troops, of which only 3,000 were German *Schutztruppen*, and the rest local African tribal warriors. He led *"the greatest single guerilla campaign in history, and the most successful"*, and remained undefeated in the field, and the only German commander who successfully invaded a part of the British Empire during the Great War.

The German hold on its African territories was frail even from the onset of the war. Von Lettow's success in the East Africa was perhaps the only major achievement for the Germans in the African Theatre. The continent and the colonies as a whole posed a string of challenges: the territories were extremely vast, and the forces few and far in between.

The German South West Africa colony was lost in 1915, German Kamerun in 1916, and German East Africa under the command of Von Lettow surrendered in 1918. With the end of the Great War, the German Colonial Empire ceased to exist, and all of its former colonies were partitioned and split between the Allied powers. With the emergence of the Third Reich and the Second World War, the Germans created new plans of regaining territories in Africa, which they never managed to implement successfully.

CHAPTER XI
OTTOMAN EMPIRE
IN THE GREAT WAR

MANY OF YOU MIGHT BE wondering: *What of the Ottoman Empire's role in the Great War?*

Well, being one of the old Empires of Europe, it was undoubtedly bound to enter the all-encompassing conflict that was the Great War. However, it is worth noting that in the late 19th and early 20th centuries, the Ottoman Empire was a mere shadow of what it once was. For years before the First World War even began, it was called the *"sick man of Europe"*.

Venerable and old-fashioned, it still had a whole lot of distance to catch up to the major European powers. While others have all largely entered the new era of industrialism and new, modern technologies, the Ottoman Empire was an agricultural nation. Moreover, it was suffering from almost a decade of rapid decline: wracked by internal strife and political instability, and by the wars and uprisings of the numerous ethnic minorities that comprised its Empire, it was generally in a very bad situation.

A major contributing factor to this weakness were the Balkan Wars led against it in 1912 and 1913. The combined nations of the Balkan League had both numerical and strategic upper hand against the Ottomans. The latter suffered a major defeat and depleted most of its resources in the process. But even before that, in 1908, the Young Turks Rebellion caused great instability in the Empire – culturally, socially, and politically. Still, it was after the rebellion came extensive reforms in the country, and that included the military as well, giving rise to the fairly modernized Ottoman army.

So, when the Great War began in 1914, the Ottoman Empire declared neutral. However, this was not to last long. It entered the war in quite the sneaky way: it carried out a surprise naval attack on the Russian Black Sea ports on October 29th 1914, causing great damage and officially joining the war on the side of the Central Powers. The Allies quickly responded by declaring war. It is still widely debated by historians as to why exactly did the Ottoman government change its mind and enter the war. The possible reasons are many – but in the end it could simply be that they hoped to turn the tide of their decline and rise up once more. Albeit, they didn't know that they joined the wrong side.

However a frail nation it might have been, the Ottoman Empire was still a considerable threat and a worthy opponent. Thus, when it entered the war on the side of the Central Powers, it placed even more strain on the powers of the Allies (Entente). It forced Russia to face this new opponent in the inhospitable mountains of the Caucasus, a further hit on their resources and military strengths. The campaign in the Caucasus was an expected one: the Ottoman Empire had a long history of pretentions on Armenia, Georgia, and other nations of this mountainous region. Ottoman Empire's main military leader, İsmail Enver Pasha, also had his gaze on a particularly juicy target: the Persian oil fields. His intention was thus to overrun Georgia, and later occupy north west regions of Persia, and the oil fields there. Alas, his lofty plan fail to materialize: the Caucasus Campaign was a big bite for them. The Russians managed to stand their ground, inflicting heavy losses on the Ottomans, especially in the Battle of Sarikamish, which the latter lost. Their casualties quickly mounted to 100,000, accumulated over several decisive battles. Further 60,000 casualties were reported during the winter of 1916-1917.

The Dardanelles Campaign was another important part of the Great War which involved the Ottoman Empire. More famously known as the Battle of Gallipoli, it was one of the bloodiest and fiercest campaigns fought in the Middle East in the First World War, and especially costly for the British, the Australians, and New Zealanders. Lasting from February 17th 1915 to January 9th 1916, it was a major effort by the Allied powers to weaken the Ottoman Empire and attempt to remove it from the war. The focus of the campaign was the Dardanelles Strait – a major strategic pass that connects a boundary between Asia and Europe. In the Great War, it would serve as a crucial passage for sending supplies to Russia.

One of the opening Allied operations of this campaign was a disaster: the Allied fleet – 18 battleships strong – attempted to force the strait and achieve dominance on the water. What happened instead was an utter failure – several ships were either badly damaged or sunk by Ottoman mines, while some were damaged from artillery.

In general, the Dardanelles Campaign was a gross understatement of the Ottoman Empire's military potentials by the Allies. Around January 1916, with the casualties dangerously high on both sides, and after a string of losses in land battles, the Allies withdrew. It was a great defeat, and costly. For the Ottomans, it became a celebrated victory, and one of the crucial moments in the future developments of the state.

Their other focus, after the Caucasus proved to be somewhat of a failure, was facing the British Army in Iran, in the Persian Campaign. This was one of the more devastating episodes of the entire Great War, and especially costly for the civilian populace of Iran. It lasted from December 14th to October 30th 1918, and ended in a stalemate, although not in Ottoman Empire's favor. Still, the campaign ended with more than 2,000,000 dead Persian civilians, who perished due to genocide and mass famine. After these generally failed campaigns, the Ottoman's slowly backed out. In 1917 and 1918, they resorted to negotiations with their enemies, seeing that their involvement in the war was certainly more of a challenge than they thought at first. The first of these negotiations was the Erzincan Armistice, signed on 5th December 1917. It brought the end of conflicts between Russia and the

Ottomans. Other negotiations soon followed, and the Ottoman Empire's representatives struggled intensely to gain at least some of their desired goals. Some of these were gained with the Treaty of Brest-Litovsk, from which they gained territories of Ardahan, Batum, and Kars. One of their lasting hostilities was that with the Christian nation of Armenia. Through this treaty though, they managed to oblige Russia to demobilize the army of Armenia, thus weakening their age-old foe.

Amongst the final of their involvements in the region and in the great war was the conflict with Armenia. Even after conducting the infamous and devastating *Armenian Genocide* against the Armenian people – in which millions perished - the Ottomans still haven't managed to vanquish this struggling nation. Thus it was that the Ottomans, using their 3rd Army, began a major offensive in Armenia in April 1918. This was followed by strong opposition from the Armenian people, and three major defeats for the Ottomans.

In the end, the effects of the Great War proved to be too much of a strain on the already affected Ottoman Empire. The process of its dissolution and demise was already underway – even before 1914. Thus, with the strain of the military engagements and the overall cost in resources and manpower, it was simply a question of time before the end of the Ottoman Empire came. The end came in 1922, after 633 long years.

CHAPTER XII
PROVOKING CONFLICT: UNITED STATES ENTER THE WAR

WE SURELY CANNOT OMIT the United States and their crucial role in the development of the First World War. But before we start this chapter, it is important to remember that at first, the popularly called *"Yanks"* remained at the sidelines. The United States adopted a role of something like an "older brother", trying to mediate a peace amongst the warring nations while itself pursuing a policy of non-intervention, due to the foreign policies of their President Woodrow Wilson.

However, several incidents suggested that an American intervention was imminent. The first such event occurred in 1915, when the German submarines sunk a British liner, the RMS *Lusitania*. Amongst those who lost their lives were 128 American citizens, which had a significant result on the American public. Woodrow Wilson nonetheless remained restrained, and declared that the United States and its people are *"too proud to fight"*. The only move he made was to insist that Germany would cease targeting civilian, passenger ships – a reasonable demand which was soon accepted.

Further attempts at brokering peace in Europe were generally seen as a failure: with the war raging fiercely across Europe and the world, these actions by Wilson were seen as futile, threatening his re-election as President of the United States. This he won barely. All the while, the German naval forces, mainly its submarines, continued their unchecked warfare, which many prominent figures likened to piracy. These actions led to repeated *warnings* by the United States that such acts that defied international law would *not* be tolerated. For the Central Powers, Germany in particular, such warnings could very well be seen as *threats.*

For the German high command, such an emphasis on submarine warfare – against both merchant, military, and passenger ships – was a direct way of weakening the British and breaking their supply lines. With the onset of 1917, they kept this strategy up, fully realizing the provocation it posed for the Americans.

One further provocation occurred with the infamous *Zimmermann Telegram*, which must be mentioned here. In it, the German Foreign Minister, Arthur Zimmermann, attempted to lure Mexico into a war against the United States, promising military support if it accepted. The telegram got intercepted by the United Kingdom – whether by chance or purpose, you decide – and presented to the United States embassy. When presented to President Wilson, and then to the American public, it created quite the effect. It was taken as a cause and provocation to war, and finally roused the United States to act. Woodrow Wilson emphasized the necessity of America entering this war: he claimed that by achieving victory, it would be a sure way to end any prospects of such conflicts emerging in the future. Now, more than a century later, we know he was far from right. In the meanwhile, the German submarines continued their ferocious submarine war, and in the process sunk seven merchant ships belonging to the United States. With this and the Zimmermann Telegram, America was finally provoked to war, which was declared to Germany on April 6th, 1917.

12.1 – Western Front's Facelift

Although it fought on, and was considered a part of, the Allied Powers, the United States were not a part of the Entente. The American public eagerly accepted the war, and soon enough, more than 2,800,000 men were drafted. Moreover, the United States cleverly decided to grant full citizenship to Puerto Rican people, drafting them too to fight in Europe.

With all these numbers combined, the Allies in Europe had a significant help in their struggle, with nearly 10,000 American soldiers entering France *daily* in 1918. The entry of America was another defining episode of the Great War as a whole, as it provided a crucial leverage for the struggling Allied forces on the Western Front, significantly changing the dynamic that was present up to that point. And not only were the Allies bolstered on land by fresh infantry, but were greatly strengthened on the sea as well, with the powerful American navy joining forces with that of the British.

The first disagreement however, soon followed. The British and the French wanted to break up the American contingents in order to patch up their battered and tattered frontlines. This would mean the breakup of American units. Realizing the strategic danger this would bring, the American General John Pershing refused to accept it.

Furthermore, the Americans oddly enough relied on very outdated tactics, which initially placed their worth into question. Pershing himself still relied on these aged strategies, often committing his forces into mass charges and full frontal attacks, suffering heavy casualties. The British and the French, who already gained substantial experience by 1918, knew that the tactic was extremely unsuccessful. Either way, the disagreements fizzled out with Pershing finding a stop-gap solution by allowing his African-American regiments to be combined with French units. Perhaps the most notorious of these was the unit known as the *Harlem Hellfighters*, officially the 369th Infantry Regiment. The nickname Hell Fighters was given to them by the Germans.

This unit spent more time in the trenches than any other American unit, and also suffered the greatest losses as well.

The role of the United States in the Great War was significant. Although militarily it was situated mostly on the Western Front, the sheer boost of supplies, funds, and resources that they provided was a key advantage for the Allies. As the situation in 1918 on the Western Front was simply put *dreadful*, the battle scarred and war weary British and French soldiers certainly greeted the new reinforcements with open arms. Furthermore, the influx of fresh Allied soldiers meant that the Germans could not possibly keep up in repairing their losses.

The first major American battle on French soil was surely the Battle of Cantigny. A key strategic attempt at reducing the penetrations made by Germans in the previous month's *Michael Offensive,* the battle was a skilled American victory, and served to greatly boost the morale of war-weary Frenchmen. This was the first attack by any American division in the war, and an opening success. Casualties on both sides were moderate, but certainly not insignificant.

The next crucial engagement for the Yanks was the Battle of Château-Thierry, a part of the wider Second Battle of the Marne. It was an Allied attempt at pushing back the previous German advance, and ended in effective American counter-offensive action. Once more the Americans relied on the success of the *rolling barrage* strategy, in which they covered territory in successive waves.

The next engagement was perhaps even more important. The Battle of Belleau Wood lasted from 1st to 26th of June 1918, and saw the exemplary service of American 2nd and 3rd Divisions. This battle was the defining achievement of the American Marines in the war, and one of the fiercest that Americans experienced. The larger-than-life feats they achieved in this battle, especially in the Assault on Hill 142 and the Belleau Woods itself, became the subject of much propaganda back home in the United States, and served as inspiration for fresh recruits. Even the Germans – who lost the battle – praised the skill and the ferocity of the Marines as fighting men. The Americans suffered nearly 10,000 casualties in this battle.

These victories combined were a defining aspect that helped the Allied forces to stop and push back the last offensive that the Germans attempted in the Great War – the *Spring Offensive of 1918*. This victory was quickly exploited, as the allies began an offensive of their own – from August to November 1918, they pushed the Germans back with rapid and fierce attacks along the entire front. This was the final Allied offensive, known as the *Hundred Days Offensive*, and one of the precursors to the one-by-one capitulation of the Central Powers. The role of the Americans in this final offensive was extremely significant. Thus the last offensive ended in victory. On 11th November 1918, the German moral finally run its course: it collapsed fully and brought the end of the war into sight. Its success caused the collapse of the Western Front and the end of the Great War.

Whether the entrance of the Americans into the Great War could be prevented by the Central Powers remains debatable: continued provocations certainly didn't help the matter. However, there is a distinct possibility that Woodrow Wilson simply bided his time, waiting to see how the Allies would fare before making his move.

Still, even after performing notably in the war, the American veterans of the Great War were faced with a difficult situation at home. Veterans received no financial aid or benefits, which resulted in mass resentment and protests later on. Moreover, America of the post-war period was one of rampant crime, social issues, corruption, and tensions. The *Prohibition of Alcohol* that began in 1920 sought to eliminate these issues or at least reduce them, but its effects are disputed, as crime and smuggling were still rampant afterwards.

And in this troubled world of post-war America, where was the battle-scarred veteran? Where were those men that charged Hill 142, the soldiers torn by the summer of 1918? In France perhaps, in their souls and minds, disillusioned by the lack of appreciation their nation showed them, taking their service and their sacrifice for granted.

CHAPTER XIII
THE BREAKDOWN:
ARMISTICES AND
CAPITULATION

WITH THE WAR IN EUROPE reaching a climactic crescendo, it was becoming clear that the end was looming. What was needed to hasten this end was a certain "chain reaction", a push that would bring about the domino-effect and the fall of the Central Powers, one by one. Before we delve deeper into the armistice itself and the German capitulation, we need to take some time to focus on that critical event that brought about the needed chain reaction.

That event is sadly often disregarded in history books, although it bears tremendous significance. It is the *Battle of Dobro Pole*, a crucial engagement that was fought between 15th and 18th September 1918, between the combined forces of Serbia, France, and Greece, against a force of Bulgarians and Germans. It was the opening stage of the wider *Vardar Offensive*, a major attack on Bulgarian forces in Vardar Macedonia.

The first attack in the battle commenced with a devastating French-Serbian artillery barrage. With a combined force of 566 guns, the bombardment had a devastating effect on Bulgarian positions.

Outnumbered and poorly equipped, the Bulgarians and their German allies had poor chances in this battle. After suffering the devastating barrage, they were faced with an all out attack from several directions. On several occasions, the Bulgarian soldier engaged in mass desertion, being unable to withstand the attacks and fleeing in every direction.

After about three days of intense fighting, the Bulgarian forces were utterly defeated, and withdrew en masse over the border, abandoning the region of Varadar Macedonia in order to protect their homeland. But it was not as simple as that. The situation within the Bulgarian army was a chaotic, mutinous disaster. Those troops that previously deserted now became mutineers, looting the Bulgarian cities of Radomir and Kyustendil, and threatening the capital of Sofia as well.

In all this chaos and confusion, a delegation of the Bulgarian high command approached the allies in Thessaloniki, asking for a possible armistice and ceasefire on 24th September 1918. After some negotiation, the French General Louis Franchet d'Esperey granted them the *Armistice of Salonica*, which was an effective surrender of the Bulgarian forces, and their removal from the First World War. Immediately after signing, their forces were disarmed and demobilized – Bulgaria was *defeated.*

The Salonica armistice was that event that precipitated the chain reaction and the eventual downfall of the enemy. It caused a complete 360 degree turn in the strategic and military balance of the Central Powers, since Germany could not effectively face its enemies without the aid of Bulgaria. Infuriated and in disbelief, the German Kaiser Wilhelm II sent an urgent telegram to the Tsar of Bulgaria, Ferdinand I. In it, he writes: *"DISGRACEFUL! 62,000 Serbs decided the war!"*

Almost immediately after Bulgaria's defeat, the then German Chancellor, Graf Georg Friedrich von Hertling, was informed by the German Supreme Army Command that the military and strategic situation in which Germany has found itself was utterly *hopeless.* The chain reaction was in full effect. The next to seek armistice was Austria-Hungary, sending its envoys to the Allies on

October 14th, 1918. The frail and failing Ottoman Empire followed in suit, seeking armistice on the following day.

For the Austro-Hungarian Empire, defeat was imminent, even before the armistice was signed. Its worn out forces were faced with a fierce Italian offensive, which ended with the Vittorio Veneto battle, after which the Austro-Hungarian army ceased to exist as a fighting force. The Empire began disintegrating at a rapid pace with this defeat. Then, when its ruling Habsburg Monarchy was overthrown, the venerable Austro-Hungarian Empire *collapsed.* From its remnants emerged two new nations, Austria and the First Hungarian Republic. Both of these countries signed separate armistices, through which numerous significant territories which were once a part of the Empire, became parts of Romania, Croatia, Serbia, Czechoslovakia, Italy, and so on.

Once the Ottoman Empire capitulated, the German Empire could see the end getting nearer. The First World War ended with the signing of the *Armistice of 11th November 1918.* This historic event occurred in a train carriage at *Le Francport* near the city of Compiègne. Those who were present and signed the armistice were the Supreme Commander of the Allies, the Marshal of France *Ferdinand Foch*; his Chief of Staff, General *Maxime Weygand;* the British First Sea Lord Admiral *Wemyss*; his deputy, Rear Admiral *George Hope*; his naval assistant, Captain *Marriott;* and on the side of the Central Powers: naval Captain *Ernst Vanselow;* Foreign Ministry representative, Graf *von Oberndorff*; Major General *von Winterfeldt*; and the politician *Matthias Erzberger*, later the Minister of Finance.

As was expected, the armistice consisted of numerous clauses, all of which were at the disadvantage of Germany. Amongst these, the most notable was the surrender of supplies and war technology: a huge part of what was in German possession. Another one was the general withdrawal of German troops from all fronts; their retreat *beyond* the Rhine, which was to be occupied by the Allies; the continuation of the Naval blockade of Germany, and numerous other terms.

The Armistice – essentially the capitulation – was signed at around 5:45 a.m., and came into effect around 11:00 a.m. that same day. Yet, even so, the fighting continued through the Western Front to the very last minute, as the confirmation of the armistice took time to reach every corner. So it was that even on the last day of the war, casualties numbered close to 11,000, of which nearly 3,000 were deaths. Amongst the more ridiculous causes of these casualties was continued artillery fire: some Allied batteries reportedly kept up the barrages in order to spend their ammo – so as not to have to haul it away.

There are two possible casualties that are considered as the "last soldier to die in the First World War". The first is the Canadian Private *George Lawrence Price*, a member of the 28th "Northwest" Battalion of Canadian Infantry. Together with his squad, Price was engaged in combat around the village of Avril on November 11th 1918. Under heavy fire from German machine gun positions, the men sought cover in the village houses. When Price stepped out onto the street, he was shot by a German sniper, hit close to the heart and killed immediately. It was 10:58 a.m., just two minutes before the armistice came into effect.

The other version – this one widely accepted – is the story of the American soldier, one Private Henry Gunther of the 313th Infantry Regiment of the 79th Division. Holding the rank of Sergeant prior to 1918, he was demoted to the rank of Private, possibly for misconduct. Anyways, with his squad, Gunther was engaged in combat around the village of Chaumont-devant-Damvillers near Meuse, where the men faced German emplacements and heavy fire. To everyone's amazement and against direct orders, Henry Gunther stood up and charged the Germans with his bayonet. No one shot at first – the Germans tried to wave him away and discourage him, as they knew of the armistice being inevitable. When Gunther didn't stop, and fired at them, they killed him instantly with machine gun fire. He died 60 seconds before the armistice. Many believed that he wanted to make a name for himself and regain his lost reputation. Instead he found death.

There is one unique detail in this story of the Great War that deserves a brief mention. For years it was a little known fact –

a true one to be sure – but recently it became an oft mentioned detail. It relates to the *Gräf & Stift Double Phaeton* automobile, in which Archduke Franz Ferdinand was assassinated. This car in which he rode when he died had the license plates which read: *"A III 118"*. Once you think about it, the license plate number directly correlates to the armistice date: A for *Armistice,* and 118 for 11.11.1918. Most regard this as a simple coincidence. Both the event that begun the Great War, and the event that ended it, having similar connecting numbers. But in a world in which there are few coincidences, this was taken as a prominent "conspiracy theory", which suggests that there might be more to it than was thought at first.

The Armistice became widely celebrated around the globe. Everyone yearned for the war's end, and hastened to rebuild their ravaged nations. Alas, in the following chapter we will learn that peace was not the end to Europe's problems – in many regards, the worst was yet to come. Nevertheless, the *Armistice Day* – November 11th – became a celebrated national holiday in many nations of Europe. One of the bloodiest, most devastating conflicts in human history, the so-called *"war to end all wars"*, was finally *over.*

CHAPTER XIV
FAR FROM FINISHED:
THE AFTERMATH
OF THE FIRST
WORLD WAR

14.1 – Crisis All Around

AS COULD BE EXPECTED in the aftershock of such a devastating and widespread global conflict, the world was never to be the same again. With the Paris Peace Conference of 1919, the war was officially ended, and Europe began a long road towards recovery, with the whole world following in its steps. But this road to peace was merely an apparition – no such thing existed in Europe in those turbulent years, and even after the Great War ended, many regions were still engaged in wars and conflicts. In the Balkans, Romania and Hungary were engaged in a bitter war, while in Albania warfare was a continuous occurrence. In the north, the Baltic states fought a difficult war to attain their independence. And in the east, in Russia, there was a whole string of leaders, movements, and bloody, merciless conflicts. So it was that Europe, after all the suffering, was still not out of the danger.

But if we focus on the Central Europe itself, where the war raged on in its full extent, we can see that the effects of the peace were to leave long lasting changes. One major change in the world after the war was the end of the major Empires of Europe. The frail Ottoman Empire didn't stand a chance of surviving the Great War, and the German, Russian, and Austro-Hungarian Empires all met their end with the war's end. This global, orchestrated downfall of the millennia old empires was one of the irreversible, biggest, and far-reaching changes with which the world was faced, and ushered us into the world in which we live today. And since these empires were consisting of numerous ethnicities and semi-independent historic territories, their disappearance meant that these "liberated" nations were now to become full-fledged countries. In the Eastern Europe, the newly liberated nations emerged: Independent Poland as the Second Polish Republic, and Czechoslovakia which gained its independence from Austria-Hungary. Further east, several incarnations of an independent Ukrainian state emerged. Furthermore, Lithuania, Latvia, and Estonia gained independence in 1918, after the Treaty of Brest-Litovsk. This independence would last until 1940. Finland too became an independent nation, and would remain so ever since, although it had to struggle and fight to remain as such.

In the aftermath of the Great War, Russia became one heavily distraught, war torn nation, experiencing wave after wave of conflict and change. The first major of these conflicts was certainly the *Russian Revolution of 1917*, a turbulent period of social upheaval and major political changes in this country. The revolution technically lasted from 1917's fall of monarchy, up to the 1923. It began with rise of the Bolshevik movement, a far-left, radical and revolutionary Marxist movement. After a violent revolution, the Bolsheviks managed to overthrow the last Russian Emperor, Nicholas II, and then murder him and his family in cold blood. This resulted in the establishment of the Soviet Union in 1922, a federal socialist state that would exist until 1992. The revolution that began in 1917 was the major contributor and a part of the wider Russian Civil War. This war saw two conflicted factions, the Bolshevik led *Red Army,* and the pro-Monarchist Russian *White Army.* The latter lost.

The Russian Civil War was one of the major conflicts in the

aftermath of the Great War, claiming some 12,000,000 total casualties, showcasing the grim and unforgiving fate that the Russian and other Slavic peoples had to endure in the 20th century. Germany, the loser of the Great War, had to face its own set of hardships in the war's aftermath. Not only was it heavily affected by the Paris Peace treaty, which limited its army to just 100,000 men, scuttled its navy, and prevented the use of tanks and other advanced technologies, but it was also facing great civil unrest. So it was, that in a scenario similar to that of Russia, the year 1918 ushered Germany in a revolution. Known as the November or German Revolution, it lasted from 1918 to 1919, and in the process, the German Empire ceased to exist. The revolution was led by the far-left, radical Social Democratic Party of Germany at the head of the so-called Weimar Republic.

In less than a year, the German Kaiser, Wilhelm II, was forced to abdicate, and the German Monarchy was completely abolished. With the communist's victory, the *Weimar Republic* was established and would last until 1933 and the rise of National Socialism. The Weimar Republic ushered Germany into a wholly new age: gone were the old habits and traditional lifestyles. Germany's capital and all large cities descended into liberal cultures, and the "Roaring Twenties" quickly took hold. Homosexualism, promiscuity, and depravity would mark this interwar period, and would only be abolished after 1933.

14.2 – Freedom With a Bitter Taste

Even for the victors, the war came at a debilitating cost. The United Kingdom felt this the most, as it almost exhausted itself by funding the war, placing a severe economic pressure on the nation. Debts accumulated and inflation soared in the post-war years. Moreover, the home industry was affected due to the reparations from Germany. The latter was obliged to provide free goods as form of *war reparation*, and such an influx directly affected British industry. Scholars often say that Britain was the nation who *"bankrupted itself in order to defeat Germany"*.

And for the Irish people too, this had significant repercussions. The ever-growing desire for independence from British Rule caused great discontent in Ireland, precipitating the 1916 *Easter Rebellion* (Éirí Amach na Cásca) which was a complete failure for Irish Republicans. This failed uprising led to a further wedge between Britain and Ireland and forced the British to attempt military conscriptions throughout Ireland, leading to a new crisis in 1918. These unrests all led to the *Irish War of Independence* (Cogadh na Saoirse), which lasted from 1919 to 1921. This crucial conflict in the aftermath of the Great War ended in a ceasefire, and the Anglo-Irish treaty which resulted in the partition of Ireland: through this partition was created the Irish Free State, a state independent from the United Kingdom, but still a part of the British Empire, and the area under direct British rule – Northern Ireland.

But even then, war and death had not left Ireland: immediately after the War of Independence, the Irish Civil War took over. Lasting from 1922 to 1923, it saw the Irish Free State forces, loyal to the treaty that was achieved, fight against the IRA, Irish Republican Army, who sought full independence from the British. The former were supplied with weapons from the British, and that helped them to gain a victory. Although defeated, the IRA continued their fight for freedom, which lasts even today.

In summary, the world map became considerably different in the aftermath of the First World War. Numerous countries gained their independence for the very first time, and this made for a quite distinct socio-political and ethno-cultural map, one that will be a crucial setting for the Second World War, which was – unbeknownst to many – not too far away.

In the distant Caucasus, Armenia first gained independence from the Russian Empire, ever since the Middle Ages, as did its close neighbor Georgia. Estonia and Finland also snatched their independence as the Russian Empire disintegrated, as did the neighboring Lithuania and Latvia.

With the collapse of Austria-Hungary, many neighboring and newly emerged states pieced out their territories: Italy took from the ruins of the Empire Trieste, South Tyrol, and Istria; Czechoslovakia claimed Moravia, parts of Silesia, and Bohemia;

Romania took control over the Hungarian parts of Banat, Maramures, and the Austrian regions of Bukovina; while the Kingdom of Serbs, Croats, and Slovenes took from Austria the Kingdom of Dalmatia and the Duchy of Carniola, and from Hungary the parts of Banat, Bacska, Baranya, and so on.

One extremely significant event in the aftermath of the war would leave deep and irreversible marks on the entire world. Known as the *Spanish Flu*, the 1918 influenza epidemic was one of the most fatal virus outbreaks in human history, and would claim close to 100 million lives. It lasted from 1918, while the Great War still raged, and until April 1920. During its run, the flu infected close to 500 million people, which at the time was one third of the entire global population. The Spanish Flu was first documented in United States, where it was diagnosed on an army cook in Camp Funston in Kansas, one Gitchell Albert, on March 4th 1918. There were further cases diagnosed in Fort Riley in Kansas, and even more in New York City. With the entry of the United States Army into the European theatre of the Great War, the virus spread rapidly, reaching France, Britain, and Germany. No one knows where the name "*Spanish* flu" emerged from – Spain at the time was a neutral country. Some sources at the time reported on the illness of the Spanish King Alfonso, and the name might have come from there. In other parts of the world, the influenza had different names, such as the "*Bolshevik Disease*" in Poland, or the "German Flu" in Brazil.

The flu spread like wildfire. By May of 1918, it had reached Poland, India, North Africa, Japan, followed by China in June, and Australia in July. In the first six months of the flu's run, the deaths were moderate – giving no cause for alarm. But it was the second wave of 1918 that really caused panic throughout the world. Hastened by the movement of troops all over the world, the flu spread with incredible haste, and was present in almost every corner of the globe. This wave was the most fatal of the whole epidemic: in roughly three months there were close to 300,000 deaths only in the United States. In India, the flu claimed close to 20 million lives just in 1918, while the capitals of Europe numbered tens of thousands of victims. In 1919, the third wave of the virus hit central Europe, claiming hundreds of thousands of deaths across several nations. It was followed by the fourth and final wave in 1920.

For the entire world, the loss of life was an enormous catastrophe. The millions of casualties of the Great War were a tragedy in itself – but it was made even worse with the additional millions of Spanish Flu victims. The United States, in which the flu possibly originated, almost 850,000 people died. Native American communities were especially affected, being more vulnerable to epidemics, and living in small communities. Entire Native villages were wiped from existence as a result. To the South, in Brazil, the death toll reached 300,000. In Europe, France lost close to 400,000 citizens, while in Britain this number was smaller – 250,000. Japan was also hit very hard by the virus: 23 million people were infected, with more than 390,000 dying as a result. The Russians were hit hard as well, with reported 450,000 deaths.

The flu had a huge impact on normal life across the world. Outbreaks impacted entire communities, especially in less developed areas, and places where there was a large difference in ages. Some towns were incapacitated with the majority of adults succumbing to the disease. Healthcare was heavily affected, as was economy. In several reported cases, the death toll was so devastatingly high that the dead could not be buried. This resulted in a number of mass graves – in which the dead were laid without coffins. Alaska is a clear example of just how devastating such an outbreak can be. Its remote communities of Inuits were heavily impacted: many of their villages were completely gone because of this. Forty percent of its entire population died in the influenza. The same went for remote communities in the Pacific, where the indigenous tribes were unable to effectively combat this threat. Pacific island nation of Nauru lost a devastating 16% of its entire population, while Tonga lost 8%. One of the worst cases was in Western Samoa. When the flu reached this group of remote islands, it infected 90% of the entire population. The death toll was debilitating: 30% of men perished, 22% of women, and 10%

of kids. Especially hard hit were regions that were also suffering from mass starvation. Iran, suffering from the Persian Famine of 1917-1919, was concurrently hit with the influenza, bringing two catastrophes at once. Close to 2,430,000 people died because of this.

All of these struggles and catastrophes give us a critical and crucial insight into the state of the world in the aftermath of the Great War. One would believe that so much death all across the world would be a sobering truth to invite peace – but it is not how the world works. The First World War had much bigger, far-reaching results, many of them more devastating than the war itself. Like the waves of an aftershock, repercussions spread across the globe, changing the fate of mankind forever. The radical economical, political, and cultural changes ushered the world into an entirely new era.

CHAPTER XV
CASUALTIES

WITHOUT A SHRED OF doubt, the Great War has an infamous reputation of being one of the deadliest conflicts in human history, a reputation upheld to this very day. With the involvement of all major nation of Europe, and the spread to all other corners of the world, the war led to the mobilization of millions of men. But it was not only the soldiers who became the victims of this terrible war – it was the civilians as well. Now, like with many other global conflicts, the official statistics tend to vary and are presented from a variety of sources. Of course, those presented by each country that was involved can tend to be biased, especially in the years immediately after the war. But even so, the scope and the devastation of the war cannot be denied – it was a true whirlwind of hate that has taken countless lives, both in youth and old age. It is widely agreed by all unbiased sources that the grand total of both civilian and military casualties in the First World War is around 40 million people. Of those, deaths account for between 15 and 22 million, with around 23 million wounded men.

Putting things in perspective, and just how devastating this war was for the civilian populations, is the number of military deaths and the civilian ones. The former number between 9 and 11 million, while the latter number between 6 and 13 million. To further deal with numbers, we can state that the Central Powers involved in the war lost roughly 4 million men, while the Allied Powers lost circa 6 million. Furthermore, sources all agree that roughly 2 million people lost their lives due to a variety of diseases that ran rampant during the war, while close to 6 million persons were proclaimed missing and presumed dead.

Due to the all-too noticeable shift in methods of warfare, and the Great War being perhaps the first true *modern* conflict, a great shift in cause of death was observed – contrary to the wars that occurred up to that point. Before this, disease was the chief contributor to death tolls in war, but with the advancements in warfare during the First World War, this cause shifted to battle casualties.

As the war affected numerous countries around the world, from Asia to Europe to Africa, some nations suffered greatly from the disproportional ratio between population numbers and military personnel count. For example, we can take Serbia, the first nation to suffer the wrath of Austria-Hungary. Kingdom of Serbia was noticeably smaller at the time, and the rapid rise of casualties in the early stages of the war took an immense toll on its populace. Combining military deaths – from which the Serbian army rapidly dwindled from around 420,000 to just 100,000 men – and the onset of the Spanish Flu and the Typhus epidemic, the Serbian nation lost a significant percentage of its general population. Sources vary, but it is agreed that the Serbian casualties constituted for 8% of all Allied losses – which, when put into perspective, makes for an immense and devastating loss for this small Balkan nation. Furthermore, Serbia lost around 29% of its entire population, and perhaps 60% of its male populace. In the war's aftermath, 500,000 children were left as orphans. Serbia is just one example of several nations that suffered such incomprehensible losses during the war – losses that would permanently reflect their futures.

And as if war wasn't enough, the world saw yet another malignant contributor to the casualties of the Great War – the Spanish Flu. This uniquely deadly pandemic influenza occurred while the war was still underway, around February 1918. It would go on for roughly two years, until April 1920, and would infect close to 500 million people all over the world. Of those, it killed between 17 and 50 million persons, making it one of the deadliest pandemics in history, and the factor that would further deepen the tragic story of human loss in the Great War, bringing the misery of the world to an entirely new level.

Massacres and genocides in the war were another major contributor to casualties. As with every war, humanity's worst aspects quickly float to the surface. The Great War was somewhat pioneering in all of this – gone was the chivalry of previous decades, and gone the slow paced warfare of the musket and cavalry era. This was a war of bitterness and deep-reaching conflicts, a war in which the accumulated displeasure of entire generations quickly erupted to show the ugly side of every man. Numerous major powers descended into the crime of ethnic cleansing as the war progressed on and took on a more chaotic side. Just one of several infamous examples is the Ottoman Empire's ethnic cleansing of the Armenian population. In its final years, the Empire carried out and organized deportation and mass executions of its Armenian populations, a direct result of long lasting ethnic tensions. Turkey organized this mass expulsion between 1914 and 1923, which resulted in circa 1.5 million Armenian deaths – one of the worst tragedies in the history of this people. The similar genocide also occurred in Greece during the same time span, also instigated by the Ottomans, which resulted in close to 750,000 Greek deaths.

During the Great War, the nationalistic tensions that ran high in the years preceding it finally came out on top, causing a major strife between certain ethnicities, and the rekindling of age long tensions that lay dormant up to that point. At the war's start, the Austro-Hungarian soldiers carried out numerous massacres in Serbia, all directed against its peaceful and agrarian populace. The unique contributing factors were many: at the time, Austria-Hungary was a multi-ethnic nation, and in its ranks there were also Croats, Slovenes, Muslims, and Hungarians, all of which harbored great hate towards Serbs. The first year of the war saw them massacring villagers they met, mostly in Western Serbia. On the other side, Eastern Serbia saw the wrath of the Bulgarian Soldiers, whose centuries old hate towards Serbs quickly took over. One infamous event is the Surdulica massacre, when the Bulgarians killed around 3,000 of Serbian men.

Those Serbs who lived for centuries in Croatia – which was a territory of Austria-Hungary – were also conscripted into the latter's army – and ordered to fight against their own kin. This caused numerous desertions by these men, who fled either to their Serbian brothers on the other side, or to the Russian forces.

Another such occurrence is the so-called Rape of Belgium, which happened in the war's earliest stages, when Germany invaded this small, neutral West European nation. Notoriously, the German's were harsh in dealing with sabotages and opposition from the conquered nation. This proved much the same in the Second World War as well. After the invasion of Belgium, they retaliated to sabotaged rail lines and similar acts of defiance by mass shooting suspects and saboteurs. They also suspected all civilians to be possible guerilla fighters, and this resulted in them massacring more than 6,500 Belgian and French civilians between August and November of 1914. The Germans also resorted to destroying numerous important and historic buildings as a form of punishment for the sabotages. Of these, the most notable was a historic university library in the city of Louvain.

War never changes. In any form, it is a chaotic display of human nature and its worst aspects. Wherever war marches, death follows suit. But in the case of the First World War, the scale became larger. Industry brought forward the weapons of mass destruction, which clashed with the over-populated nations of Europe. In a grotesque mixture of old and new, death came out as the reigning champion. Littered were the fields of Europa, but not with crops and seeds and trees, but rather with blood of the innocents and the bones of the young. And even today, as I write this, the steppes of Ukraine and the hills of the Carpathians; the waters of the Pacific and the hot sands of Africa; the fields of

Flanders and the valleys of France: they are all filled with dreams and hopes, with long lost loves and unfinished letters; with broken brights and unsaid goodbyes. All of which once belonged – *to the young sons of Europa.*

CONCLUSION

WRITING THIS BOOK, constant care was taken to address only the affirmed literary and historic sources, finding the most important and concise contents to deliver to you, the reader. But history aside: Battles were won and lost; offensives failed and repulsed; Generals replaced and retired; Nations formed and dissolved. They are all insignificant when compared to the lives lost in this *war to end all wars*, which only proved to be the *first* such global conflict.

And as descendants of veterans, as mute witnesses of this devastating violence that engulfed the world a century or so ago, we are required to be worthy of the dead. To try and ask the *critical* questions, as we try to piece the puzzle of the wanton death and destruction that has claimed so many lives and so many of our own ancestors. Through our fallen forebears, or very own blood is spilled on those fields – shall we stand silent as it seeps into the ground and into memory? Silence be damned: it is the age of information. With that being said, we need to ask ourselves was it worth it? Was so much suffering asked for?

We can only reflect on the events of the Great War bitterly considering the mechanisms of the world around us. An unjust and unfair world. A world in which the young men and women, filled with desire and love and passion for *living life,* were forced to *die* in the muddy battlefields of France for whims of Emperors and Generals, and for the sake of redrawn lines on the map. What of them? *What of the doomed youth?*

> *"I dreamed kind Jesus fouled the big-gun gears;*
> *And caused a permanent stoppage in all bolts;*

And buckled with a smile Mausers and Colts;
And rusted every bayonet with His tears.
And there were no more bombs, of ours or Theirs,
Not even an old flint-lock, not even a pikel.
But God was vexed, and gave all power to Michael;
And when I woke he'd seen to our repairs."
Written in 1917 by Wilfred Owen, poet of the Great War;
Killed in action on November 4th*, 1918, one*
week before the end of the war.

Printed in Poland
by Amazon Fulfillment
Poland Sp. z o.o., Wrocław
30 October 2023

cc409f91-c188-452b-b945-86e6d3c5057aR01